D1414084

RENEW

▼

90 Days

of Spiritual Refreshment

Paul Chappell

Copyright © 2015 by Striving Together Publications. All Scripture quotations are taken from the King James Version.

First published in 2015 by Striving Together Publications, a ministry of Lancaster Baptist Church, Lancaster, CA 93535. Striving Together Publications is committed to providing tried, trusted, and proven books that will further equip local churches to carry out the Great Commission. Your comments and suggestions are valued.

All rights reserved. No part of this book may be reproduced, stored in a retrieval system, or transmitted in any form or by any means—electronic, mechanical, photocopy, recording, or otherwise—without written permission of the publisher, except for brief quotations in printed reviews.

Striving Together Publications
4020 E. Lancaster Blvd.
Lancaster, CA 93535
800.201.7748

Cover design by Andrew Jones
Layout by Craig Parker
Edited by Robert Byers and Monica Bass

The contents of this book are the result of decades of spiritual growth in life and ministry. It is not our intent to claim originality with any quote or thought that could not readily be tied to an original source.

ISBN 978–1-59894–308–5
Printed in the United States of America

Table of Contents

A Note from the Author

Dear Friend,

Have you ever started the day empty?
Depleted?
Weary?
Burdened?
Dry?
Welcome to the club.

Anyone who has served the Lord for any length of time has experienced spiritual fatigue or exhaustion. After all, we're only human. That's why God doesn't ask us to serve Him in our own strength.

In fact, He promises to renew our strength as we wait on Him. Isaiah 40:31 says, "But they that wait upon the LORD shall renew their strength; they shall mount up with wings as eagles; they shall run, and not be weary; and they shall walk, and not faint."

The best—and the only lasting—sources of renewal for God's people are the presence of God and the Word of God. The Apostle Paul wrote, "For which cause we faint not; but though our outward man perish, yet the inward man is renewed day by day" (2 Corinthians 4:16).

The ninety devotions in this book are written to encourage you to seek God's face and renew your heart in His Word. Each devotion includes a Scripture passage and provides an encouraging or admonishing truth regarding the Christian life. At the close of each devotion, you will find a single actionable thought given as "Today's Renewal Principle." Additionally, you'll find a Bible reading schedule at the bottom of each devotion that will lead you through the New Testament in ninety days.

The evangelist William Booth once said, "Look well to the fire of your soul, for it is the tendency of fire to go out." *Renew* is written to help you stir your love for the Lord and your fervency to know Him more and serve Him better. I encourage you to read these devotions with your Bible open and your heart prepared to respond to God's truth.

I pray *Renew* will encourage you to look to the Lord and live with a heart renewed in His promises.

Sincerely in Christ,

Paul Chappell

BIBLE READING SCHEDULES

▼

One-Year Bible Reading Schedule

January

☐	1	Gen. 1–3	Matt. 1
☐	2	Gen. 4–6	Matt. 2
☐	3	Gen. 7–9	Matt. 3
☐	4	Gen. 10–12	Matt. 4
☐	5	Gen. 13–15	Matt. 5:1–26
☐	6	Gen. 16–17	Matt. 5:27–48
☐	7	Gen. 18–19	Matt. 6:1–18
☐	8	Gen. 20–22	Matt. 6:19–34
☐	9	Gen. 23–24	Matt. 7
☐	10	Gen. 25–26	Matt. 8:1–17
☐	11	Gen. 27–28	Matt. 8:18–34
☐	12	Gen. 29–30	Matt. 9:1–17
☐	13	Gen. 31–32	Matt. 9:18–38
☐	14	Gen. 33–35	Matt. 10:1–20
☐	15	Gen. 36–38	Matt. 10:21–42
☐	16	Gen. 39–40	Matt. 11
☐	17	Gen. 41–42	Matt. 12:1–23
☐	18	Gen. 43–45	Matt. 12:24–50
☐	19	Gen. 46–48	Matt. 13:1–30
☐	20	Gen. 49–50	Matt. 13:31–58
☐	21	Ex. 1–3	Matt. 14:1–21
☐	22	Ex. 4–6	Matt. 14:22–36
☐	23	Ex. 7–8	Matt. 15:1–20
☐	24	Ex. 9–11	Matt. 15:21–39
☐	25	Ex. 12–13	Matt. 16
☐	26	Ex. 14–15	Matt. 17
☐	27	Ex. 16–18	Matt. 18:1–20
☐	28	Ex. 19–20	Matt. 18:21–35
☐	29	Ex. 21–22	Matt. 19
☐	30	Ex. 23–24	Matt. 20:1–16
☐	31	Ex. 25–26	Matt. 20:17–34

February

☐	1	Ex. 27–28	Matt. 21:1–22
☐	2	Ex. 29–30	Matt. 21:23–46
☐	3	Ex. 31–33	Matt. 22:1–22
☐	4	Ex. 34–35	Matt. 22:23–46
☐	5	Ex. 36–38	Matt. 23:1–22
☐	6	Ex. 39–40	Matt. 23:23–39
☐	7	Lev. 1–3	Matt. 24:1–28
☐	8	Lev. 4–5	Matt. 24:29–51
☐	9	Lev. 6–7	Matt. 25:1–30
☐	10	Lev. 8–10	Matt. 25:31–46
☐	11	Lev. 11–12	Matt. 26:1–25
☐	12	Lev. 13	Matt. 26:26–50
☐	13	Lev. 14	Matt. 26:51–75
☐	14	Lev. 15–16	Matt. 27:1–26
☐	15	Lev. 17–18	Matt. 27:27–50
☐	16	Lev. 19–20	Matt. 27:51–66
☐	17	Lev. 21–22	Matt. 28
☐	18	Lev. 23–24	Mark 1:1–22
☐	19	Lev. 25	Mark 1:23–45
☐	20	Lev. 26–27	Mark 2
☐	21	Num. 1–2	Mark 3:1–19
☐	22	Num. 3–4	Mark 3:20–35
☐	23	Num. 5–6	Mark 4:1–20
☐	24	Num. 7–8	Mark 4:21–41
☐	25	Num. 9–11	Mark 5:1–20
☐	26	Num. 12–14	Mark 5:21–43
☐	27	Num. 15–16	Mark 6:1–29
☐	28	Num. 17–19	Mark 6:30–56

March

☐	1	Num. 20–22	Mark 7:1–13
☐	2	Num. 23–25	Mark 7:14–37
☐	3	Num. 26–28	Mark 8
☐	4	Num. 29–31	Mark 9:1–29
☐	5	Num. 32–34	Mark 9:30–50
☐	6	Num. 35–36	Mark 10:1–31
☐	7	Deut. 1–3	Mark 10:32–52
☐	8	Deut. 4–6	Mark 11:1–18
☐	9	Deut. 7–9	Mark 11:19–33
☐	10	Deut. 10–12	Mark 12:1–27
☐	11	Deut. 13–15	Mark 12:28–44
☐	12	Deut. 16–18	Mark 13:1–20
☐	13	Deut. 19–21	Mark 13:21–37
☐	14	Deut. 22–24	Mark 14:1–26
☐	15	Deut. 25–27	Mark 14:27–53
☐	16	Deut. 28–29	Mark 14:54–72
☐	17	Deut. 30–31	Mark 15:1–25
☐	18	Deut. 32–34	Mark 15:26–47
☐	19	Josh. 1–3	Mark 16
☐	20	Josh. 4–6	Luke 1:1–20
☐	21	Josh. 7–9	Luke 1:21–38
☐	22	Josh. 10–12	Luke 1:39–56
☐	23	Josh. 13–15	Luke 1:57–80
☐	24	Josh. 16–18	Luke 2:1–24
☐	25	Josh. 19–21	Luke 2:25–52
☐	26	Josh. 22–24	Luke 3
☐	27	Judges 1–3	Luke 4:1–30
☐	28	Judges 4–6	Luke 4:31–44
☐	29	Judges 7–8	Luke 5:1–16
☐	30	Judges 9–10	Luke 5:17–39
☐	31	Judges 11–12	Luke 6:1–26

April

☐	1	Judges 13–15	Luke 6:27–49
☐	2	Judges 16–18	Luke 7:1–30
☐	3	Judges 19–21	Luke 7:31–50
☐	4	Ruth 1–4	Luke 8:1–25
☐	5	1 Sam. 1–3	Luke 8:26–56
☐	6	1 Sam. 4–6	Luke 9:1–17
☐	7	1 Sam. 7–9	Luke 9:18–36
☐	8	1 Sam. 10–12	Luke 9:37–62
☐	9	1 Sam. 13–14	Luke 10:1–24
☐	10	1 Sam. 15–16	Luke 10:25–42
☐	11	1 Sam. 17–18	Luke 11:1–28
☐	12	1 Sam. 19–21	Luke 11:29–54
☐	13	1 Sam. 22–24	Luke 12:1–31
☐	14	1 Sam. 25–26	Luke 12:32–59
☐	15	1 Sam. 27–29	Luke 13:1–22
☐	16	1 Sam. 30–31	Luke 13:23–35
☐	17	2 Sam. 1–2	Luke 14:1–24
☐	18	2 Sam. 3–5	Luke 14:25–35
☐	19	2 Sam. 6–8	Luke 15:1–10
☐	20	2 Sam. 9–11	Luke 15:11–32
☐	21	2 Sam. 12–13	Luke 16
☐	22	2 Sam. 14–15	Luke 17:1–19
☐	23	2 Sam. 16–18	Luke 17:20–37
☐	24	2 Sam. 19–20	Luke 18:1–23
☐	25	2 Sam. 21–22	Luke 18:24–43
☐	26	2 Sam. 23–24	Luke 19:1–27
☐	27	1 Kings 1–2	Luke 19:28–48
☐	28	1 Kings 3–5	Luke 20:1–26
☐	29	1 Kings 6–7	Luke 20:27–47
☐	30	1 Kings 8–9	Luke 21:1–19

May

☐	1	1 Kings 10–11	Luke 21:20–38
☐	2	1 Kings 12–13	Luke 22:1–30
☐	3	1 Kings 14–15	Luke 22:31–46
☐	4	1 Kings 16–18	Luke 22:47–71
☐	5	1 Kings 19–20	Luke 23:1–25
☐	6	1 Kings 21–22	Luke 23:26–56
☐	7	2 Kings 1–3	Luke 24:1–35
☐	8	2 Kings 4–6	Luke 24:36–53
☐	9	2 Kings 7–9	John 1:1–28
☐	10	2 Kings 10–12	John 1:29–51
☐	11	2 Kings 13–14	John 2
☐	12	2 Kings 15–16	John 3:1–18
☐	13	2 Kings 17–18	John 3:19–36
☐	14	2 Kings 19–21	John 4:1–30
☐	15	2 Kings 22–23	John 4:31–54
☐	16	2 Kings 24–25	John 5:1–24
☐	17	1 Chr. 1–3	John 5:25–47
☐	18	1 Chr. 4–6	John 6:1–21
☐	19	1 Chr. 7–9	John 6:22–44
☐	20	1 Chr. 10–12	John 6:45–71
☐	21	1 Chr. 13–15	John 7:1–27
☐	22	1 Chr. 16–18	John 7:28–53
☐	23	1 Chr. 19–21	John 8:1–27
☐	24	1 Chr. 22–24	John 8:28–59
☐	25	1 Chr. 25–27	John 9:1–23
☐	26	1 Chr. 28–29	John 9:24–41
☐	27	2 Chr. 1–3	John 10:1–23
☐	28	2 Chr. 4–6	John 10:24–42
☐	29	2 Chr. 7–9	John 11:1–29
☐	30	2 Chr. 10–12	John 11:30–57
☐	31	2 Chr. 13–14	John 12:1–26

June

☐	1	2 Chr. 15–16	John 12:27–50
☐	2	2 Chr. 17–18	John 13:1–20
☐	3	2 Chr. 19–20	John 13:21–38
☐	4	2 Chr. 21–22	John 14
☐	5	2 Chr. 23–24	John 15
☐	6	2 Chr. 25–27	John 16
☐	7	2 Chr. 28–29	John 17
☐	8	2 Chr. 30–31	John 18:1–18
☐	9	2 Chr. 32–33	John 18:19–40
☐	10	2 Chr. 34–36	John 19:1–22
☐	11	Ezra 1–2	John 19:23–42
☐	12	Ezra 3–5	John 20
☐	13	Ezra 6–8	John 21
☐	14	Ezra 9–10	Acts 1
☐	15	Neh. 1–3	Acts 2:1–21
☐	16	Neh. 4–6	Acts 2:22–47
☐	17	Neh. 7–9	Acts 3
☐	18	Neh. 10–11	Acts 4:1–22
☐	19	Neh. 12–13	Acts 4:23–37
☐	20	Esther 1–2	Acts 5:1–21
☐	21	Esther 3–5	Acts 5:22–42
☐	22	Esther 6–8	Acts 6
☐	23	Esther 9–10	Acts 7:1–21
☐	24	Job 1–2	Acts 7:22–43
☐	25	Job 3–4	Acts 7:44–60
☐	26	Job 5–7	Acts 8:1–25
☐	27	Job 8–10	Acts 8:26–40
☐	28	Job 11–13	Acts 9:1–21
☐	29	Job 14–16	Acts 9:22–43
☐	30	Job 17–19	Acts 10:1–23

90-Day Bible Reading Schedule

Day	Start	End	✔	Day	Start	End	✔
1	Genesis 1:1	Genesis 16:16	❑	46	Proverbs 7:1	Proverbs 20:21	❑
2	Genesis 17:1	Genesis 28:19	❑	47	Proverbs 20:22	Ecclesiastes 2:26	❑
3	Genesis 28:20	Genesis 40:11	❑	48	Ecclesiastes 3:1	Song 8:14	❑
4	Genesis 40:12	Genesis 50:26	❑	49	Isaiah 1:1	Isaiah 13:22	❑
5	Exodus 1:1	Exodus 15:18	❑	50	Isaiah 14:1	Isaiah 28:29	❑
6	Exodus 15:19	Exodus 28:43	❑	51	Isaiah 29:1	Isaiah 41:18	❑
7	Exodus 29:1	Exodus 40:38	❑	52	Isaiah 41:19	Isaiah 52:12	❑
8	Leviticus 1:1	Leviticus 14:32	❑	53	Isaiah 52:13	Isaiah 66:18	❑
9	Leviticus 14:33	Leviticus 26:26	❑	54	Isaiah 66:19	Jeremiah 10:13	❑
10	Leviticus 26:27	Numbers 8:14	❑	55	Jeremiah 10:14	Jeremiah 23:8	❑
11	Numbers 8:15	Numbers 21:7	❑	56	Jeremiah 23:9	Jeremiah 33:22	❑
12	Numbers 21:8	Numbers 32:19	❑	57	Jeremiah 33:23	Jeremiah 47:7	❑
13	Numbers 32:20	Deuteronomy 7:26	❑	58	Jeremiah 48:1	Lamentations 1:22	❑
14	Deuteronomy 8:1	Deuteronomy 23:11	❑	59	Lamentations 2:1	Ezekiel 12:20	❑
15	Deuteronomy 23:12	Deuteronomy 34:12	❑	60	Ezekiel 12:21	Ezekiel 23:39	❑
16	Joshua 1:1	Joshua 14:15	❑	61	Ezekiel 23:40	Ezekiel 35:15	❑
17	Joshua 15:1	Judges 3:27	❑	62	Ezekiel 36:1	Ezekiel 47:12	❑
18	Judges 3:28	Judges 15:12	❑	63	Ezekiel 47:13	Daniel 8:27	❑
19	Judges 15:13	1 Samuel 2:29	❑	64	Daniel 9:1	Hosea 13:6	❑
20	1 Samuel 2:30	1 Samuel 15:35	❑	65	Hosea 13:7	Amos 9:10	❑
21	1 Samuel 16:1	1 Samuel 28:19	❑	66	Amos 9:11	Nahum 3:19	❑
22	1 Samuel 28:20	2 Samuel 12:10	❑	67	Habakkuk 1:1	Zechariah 10:12	❑
23	2 Samuel 12:11	2 Samuel 22:18	❑	68	Zechariah 11:1	Matthew 4:25	❑
24	2 Samuel 22:19	1 Kings 7:37	❑	69	Matthew 5:1	Matthew 15:39	❑
25	1 Kings 7:38	1 Kings 16:20	❑	70	Matthew 16:1	Matthew 26:56	❑
26	1 Kings 16:21	2 Kings 4:37	❑	71	Matthew 26:57	Mark 9:13	❑
27	2 Kings 4:38	2 Kings 15:26	❑	72	Mark 9:14	Luke 1:80	❑
28	2 Kings 15:27	2 Kings 25:30	❑	73	Luke 2:1	Luke 9:62	❑
29	1 Chronicles 1:1	1 Chronicles 9:44	❑	74	Luke 10:1	Luke 20:19	❑
30	1 Chronicles 10:1	1 Chronicles 23:32	❑	75	Luke 20:20	John 5:47	❑
31	1 Chronicles 24:1	2 Chronicles 7:10	❑	76	John 6:1	John 15:17	❑
32	2 Chronicles 7:11	2 Chronicles 23:15	❑	77	John 15:18	Acts 6:7	❑
33	2 Chronicles 23:16	2 Chronicles 35:15	❑	78	Acts 6:8	Acts 16:37	❑
34	2 Chronicles 35:16	Ezra 10:44	❑	79	Acts 16:38	Acts 28:16	❑
35	Nehemiah 1:1	Nehemiah 13:14	❑	80	Acts 28:17	Romans 14:23	❑
36	Nehemiah 13:15	Job 7:21	❑	81	Romans 15:1	1 Corinthians 14:40	❑
37	Job 8:1	Job 24:25	❑	82	1 Corinthians 15:1	Galatians 3:25	❑
38	Job 25:1	Job 41:34	❑	83	Galatians 3:26	Colossians 4:18	❑
39	Job 42:1	Psalms 24:10	❑	84	1 Thessalonians 1:1	Philemon 25	❑
40	Psalms 25:1	Psalms 45:14	❑	85	Hebrews 1:1	James 3:12	❑
41	Psalms 45:15	Psalms 69:21	❑	86	James 3:13	3 John 14	❑
42	Psalms 69:22	Psalms 89:13	❑	87	Jude 1	Revelation 17:18	❑
43	Psalms 89:14	Psalms 108:13	❑	88	Revelation 18:1	Revelation 22:21	❑
44	Psalms 109:1	Psalms 134:3	❑	89	Grace Day	Grace Day	❑
45	Psalms 135:1	Proverbs 6:35	❑	90	Grace Day	Grace Day	❑

DEVOTIONS

▼

The Urgent Need for Renewal

Even the youths shall faint and be weary, And the young men shall utterly fall: But they that wait upon the Lord shall renew their strength; They shall mount up with wings as eagles; They shall run, and not be weary; And they shall walk, and not faint.—**Isaiah 40:30–31**

Over the years as I have traveled across the country, I have had the opportunity to visit some of the truly great churches of the past. These were churches that were once great lighthouses—places where many were saved, where believers grew in grace, and where deep roots of faith were established. Yet sadly it is often the case that the buildings are only a shell of what was once a vibrant assembly of Christians. Some of these great auditoriums are no longer churches at all, while others have been taken over by false teachers who deny the truths once proclaimed from those pulpits.

What causes these tragedies? What makes churches or individual Christians stop walking with God and turn aside after other things? What leads to the failure to finish strong? While there are many causes, one of the most common is that people and organizations fail to be renewed. As a result, their strength wanes, and then they collapse. The reality is that we are constantly facing threats and challenges that are beyond what we can meet in our own strength.

Paul wrote, "For which cause we faint not; but though our outward man perish, yet the inward man is renewed day by day" (2 Corinthians 4:16). The devil knows that if he can convince us to do good works in our own strength rather than through the power of the Holy Spirit, he has placed our feet on the road to ruin. Rather than relying on ourselves, we should be running to the Lord daily for a renewal of our strength.

—— Today's Renewal Principle ——

We need to regularly go to God and spend time in His Word, looking to Him to renew our strength.

Listening for God's Voice

*And the LORD called Samuel again the third time.
And he arose and went to Eli, and said, Here am I;
for thou didst call me. And Eli perceived that the
LORD had called the child. Therefore Eli said unto
Samuel, Go, lie down: and it shall be, if he call
thee, that thou shalt say, Speak, LORD; for thy
servant heareth. So Samuel went and lay down in
his place.*—**1 Samuel 3:8–9**

I read about a naturalist and his friend who were
walking through a New York City park. At one
point the naturalist said to his friend, "Did you
hear that cricket?" His friend replied, "With all the
noise in this park how do you hear a cricket?" The
naturalist said, "You hear what you train yourself
to hear." To prove his point, he took some coins
from his pocket and threw them on the sidewalk.
Everyone nearby immediately stopped and looked.

If we are going to walk with God in the midst of
a society that is going the other direction, we must
hear His voice. There will always be other voices

calling out to distract us from our course, but our ears should be open and eager to hear what God has to say. This is what James had in mind when he instructed us to "be swift to hear" (James 1:19).

Though the world speaks loudly, God often whispers. This was the experience Elijah had when he was running for his life from Jezebel. Alone on a mountain, he witnessed loud and powerful events: "And after the earthquake a fire; but the Lord was not in the fire: and after the fire a still small voice" (1 Kings 19:12). Hearing that "still small voice" is vital to the renewal of our strength for the Christian walk day after day, but it does not happen unless we are willing to focus our hearing to discover what God has to say.

—— Today's Renewal Principle ——

Be sensitive to God's voice so you receive His instruction and encouragement for daily living.

It Should Disturb Us

Now while Paul waited for them at Athens, his spirit was stirred in him, when he saw the city wholly given to idolatry. Therefore disputed he in the synagogue with the Jews, and with the devout persons, and in the market daily with them that met with him.—**Acts 17:16–17**

On January 13, 2012, the massive *Costa Concordia* cruise ship with more than 4,200 passengers and crew on board was sailing off the coast of Italy on a tour of the Mediterranean Sea. The captain deviated from his planned course, and the ship struck a reef near the shore. After taking on water for a while, the ship began to sink. Going against centuries of tradition and abandoning responsibility, Captain Francesco Schettino left the ship instead of remaining to make sure everyone could be rescued.

In a phone conversation, the local Coast Guard commander pressed Schettino for an update on the situation. "Tell me if there are women, children and people in need there." Failing to receive a satisfactory reply, he ordered Schettino to return to the ship. The captain responded, "You realize it's dark and we can't see anything?" "You've been telling me that for an hour, now get back on board!" the official shouted. The captain was later arrested for his failure to do his duty, resulting in the deaths of more than thirty people.

Every day we are surrounded by people who will spend eternity either in Heaven or in Hell. The fact that so many are lost should disturb us. The Bible tells us that Jesus cared about the people a great deal. "But when he saw the multitudes, he was moved with compassion on them, because they fainted, and were scattered abroad, as sheep having no shepherd" (Matthew 9:36). Let your heart be stirred by the condition of the lost, and do everything you can to win others to Christ.

—— **Today's Renewal Principle** ——

As you walk through the world, let the lost condition of the men and women you meet stir compassion in your heart.

The Blessing of Right Delight

Blessed is the man that walketh not in the counsel of the ungodly, nor standeth in the way of sinners, nor sitteth in the seat of the scornful. But his delight is in the law of the Lord; And in his law doth he meditate day and night. And he shall be like a tree planted by the rivers of water, That bringeth forth his fruit in his season; His leaf also shall not wither; And whatsoever he doeth shall prosper.—**Psalm 1:1–3**

Few people will admit that they want to be miserable. Most say they want to be happy. Yet if you know very many people at all, you realize that a lot of people are not happy. Part of the reason for that is that so many people seek their delight in the wrong places. When we delight in things that are temporary, even good things, we, at best, have fleeting happiness. When we delight in things that are eternal, we can enjoy happiness regardless of our circumstances.

We see a clear illustration of this during the ministry of Jesus. Luke 10 records that He sent seventy of His followers out two by two to preach and minister. Before He sent them out, He gave them power to perform miracles of healing and to deliver people from demons. When they returned, these disciples were thrilled and were rejoicing at what they had experienced. But Jesus said, "Notwithstanding in this rejoice not, that the spirits are subject unto you; but rather rejoice, because your names are written in heaven" (Luke 10:20).

The principle for us is that we need to walk each day with our hearts fixed on that which is eternal. When our delight is in the Word of God, His gift of salvation, and our future in Heaven we can keep a spirit of rejoicing no matter what happens because our delight is in the right things.

—— Today's Renewal Principle ——

If you want to experience God's blessings, learn to delight in the things in which He delights.

Let Us Kneel

O come, let us sing unto the LORD: let us make a joyful noise to the rock of our salvation. Let us come before his presence with thanksgiving, and make a joyful noise unto him with psalms. For the LORD is a great God, and a great King above all gods. In his hand are the deep places of the earth: the strength of the hills is his also. The sea is his, and he made it: and his hands formed the dry land. O come, let us worship and bow down: let us kneel before the LORD our maker.—**Psalm 95:1–6**

Even as a baby, Jesus inspired worship. When the wise men came to see Him, they knelt in His presence. After the shepherds had seen Him, they spread praise to God across the countryside. When Anna and Simeon saw Him in the temple, they lifted their voices in thanks to God. The pattern continued throughout Jesus' adult life and ministry. Peter knelt before Him in the fishing boat. The lepers knelt before Him and begged to be healed. Again and again, we see people before Jesus on their knees.

The word *worship* is a combination word from Old English "worth-ship" meaning something is of great value and worthy to be honored. That is Jesus. He alone deserves the praise, worship, and adoration of our hearts. Today it seems that we put everything else in the place that rightfully belongs to God. We follow after fleeting and temporal things of no real value. We allow our selfish desires to direct our actions instead of obeying God's commands.

All of this would change if we saw Jesus for who He really is. If we truly understand His glory and greatness, we will find ourselves on our knees before Him, willing to do exactly as He directs. There is a strong bond between worship and obedience. Jesus said, "If ye love me, keep my commandments" (John 14:15).

—— Today's Renewal Principle ——

Reflecting on the majesty and glory of Jesus should drive us to our knees in worship before Him.

Finding Hope in the Storms

And he arose, and rebuked the wind, and said unto the sea, Peace, be still. And the wind ceased, and there was a great calm. And he said unto them, Why are ye so fearful? how is it that ye have no faith? And they feared exceedingly, and said one to another, What manner of man is this, that even the wind and the sea obey him?—**Mark 4:39–41**

Annie Johnson Flint knew a great deal about suffering and hardship. Her mother died when she was just three, and her father died while she was also young. A loving Christian family adopted Annie and her sister, and then that couple died as well. In her twenties, Annie was working as a school teacher when she was stricken by crippling arthritis from which she never recovered. Making ends meet was a constant struggle. Yet, even with all that Annie Flint endured, she never lost her faith and hope in God. One of her best-known poems is "What God Has Promised."

> *God has not promised skies always blue,*
> *Flower-strewn pathways all our life through;*

God has not promised sun without rain,
Joy without sorrow, peace without pain.
But God has promised strength for the day,
Rest for the labor, light for the way;
Grace for the trials, help from above,
Unfailing sympathy, undying love.

When the disciples were caught in a terrible storm and feared for their lives (remember that several of them had spent their adult lives on the water and knew the difference between a regular storm and a threatening one), they cried out to Jesus in terror. After He calmed the storm, Jesus rebuked them for being afraid. While fear is a natural reaction to trouble and storms, it is the wrong reaction. Instead, our hope should see the presence of God as our security and rest in Him.

—— Today's Renewal Principle ——

Remember the unfailing promises of God to never leave or forsake you, and you will find hope even amid your storms.

Standing Strong in Opposition

*For I will not see you now by the way; but I trust
to tarry a while with you, if the Lord permit. But
I will tarry at Ephesus until Pentecost. For a great
door and effectual is opened unto me, and there
are many adversaries.*—**1 Corinthians 16:7–9**

When he was appointed as the pastor of a
church in Cambridge, England, in 1783,
Charles Simeon was delighted. The people of the
church, however, did not share his joy. Many of
the prominent members opposed his convictions
on reaching the lost with the gospel. To show their
displeasure, they locked their pew boxes during the
service and left them empty so that those who came
to hear Simeon preach had to stand or sit in the
aisles. Eventually, God began to work, and Simeon's
ministry had a powerful influence on the nation
of England and the world through his efforts to
encourage missionary work.

During the dark days of opposition, Simeon
wrote, "In this state of things I saw no remedy but
faith and patience....It was painful indeed to see

the church, with the exception of the aisles, almost forsaken; but I thought that if God would only give a double blessing to the congregation that did attend, there would on the whole be as much good done as if the congregation were doubled and the blessing limited to only half the amount. This comforted me many, many times, when without such a reflection, I should have sunk under my burden."

Opposition does not mean that we are doing things wrong. Often it is evidence that we are doing things right. If we allow ourselves to be deterred from doing anything unless we have complete approval, it is certain that we will never accomplish anything of value. Rather than being discouraged by opposition, we should take comfort in God's faithfulness and keep doing what is right.

—— Today's Renewal Principle ——

Be strong in the Lord; no great work for God has ever been done without opposition from the enemy.

Love and Peaceful Living

Let love be without dissimulation. Abhor that which is evil; cleave to that which is good. Be kindly affectioned one to another with brotherly love; in honour preferring one another; Recompense to no man evil for evil. Provide things honest in the sight of all men. If it be possible, as much as lieth in you, live peaceably with all men.—**Romans 12:9–10, 17–18**

Abraham Lincoln won the presidency of a divided country. In 1860, Lincoln narrowly received his electoral majority. Among his harshest critics was Edwin Stanton of Ohio who opposed Lincoln's election, yet Lincoln asked Stanton to serve as Secretary of War, recognizing his organizational skills were greatly needed for the war effort. When Lincoln was assassinated, Stanton said, "There lies the most perfect ruler of men the world has ever seen."

We do not have to strike back at everyone who says or does something we disagree with. It may be temporarily satisfying, but in the end it leads to bitterness and often an escalating cycle of revenge and retaliatory actions. Love does not insist on getting even; in fact, it glories in peace. Paul wrote that love "Doth not behave itself unseemly, seeketh not her own, is not easily provoked, thinketh no evil" (1 Corinthians 13:5). Many people find themselves living stress-filled lives because they do not allow love to do its work of peace.

There will always be disappointments and disagreements in life. Even the people we are closest to are not perfect and will fail us, just as we will fail them. The choice is whether in love we choose to overlook those faults or whether we allow anger to rule our hearts and insist on getting even. No one who takes the path of vengance will find rest and peace. It is guaranteed to produce resentment and bitterness.

—— Today's Renewal Principle ——

Let love overrule your desire to take vengeance, and you will lead a more peaceful life.

Picking up the Towel

Jesus knowing that the Father had given all things into his hands, and that he was come from God, and went to God; He riseth from supper, and laid aside his garments; and took a towel, and girded himself. After that he poureth water into a bason, and began to wash the disciples' feet, and to wipe them with the towel wherewith he was girded.—**John 13:3–5**

I read about a missionary who was visiting a religious festival in Brazil. As he went from booth to booth examining the different items for sale, he saw one with a sign that said, "Cheap Crosses." He thought to himself, "That's what many Christians are looking for these days—cheap crosses. My Lord's cross was not cheap. Why should mine be?"

There is no version of Bible Christianity that does not come with a cost. Dr. John Henry Jowett wrote, "Ministry that costs nothing accomplishes nothing." Jesus said "And whosoever doth not bear his cross, and come after me, cannot be my disciple" (Luke 14:27). In the Upper Room the night before

He was crucified, Jesus washed the disciples' feet. This was a dirty and disgusting job—one usually reserved for slaves to perform. Yet the Lord of Heaven and Earth was willing to wash the feet of His followers, including the feet of Judas who was about to betray Him.

Jesus did not think that menial tasks were beneath Him, yet pride tempts us to think that we deserve easy tasks that will bring us praise and glory. God is looking for people who will humble themselves and pick up a towel to serve Him by serving others. In truth, the work that you do for God may go unnoticed during your lifetime. Your name may never be well known. You may not receive acclaim and applause. But God will see, and His words "Well done" (Matthew 25:21) will be reward enough.

—— Today's Renewal Principle ——

We must be willing to pay the price of service if we want to follow the pattern Jesus set for us.

Our Hope of Heaven

And if Christ be not raised, your faith is vain; ye are yet in your sins. Then they also which are fallen asleep in Christ are perished. If in this life only we have hope in Christ, we are of all men most miserable. But now is Christ risen from the dead, and become the firstfruits of them that slept.—**1 Corinthians 15:17–20**

The truth of the resurrection is the foundation of the Christian faith. If the resurrection of Christ is not a reality, we have no hope for this life or the next. Because Jesus died and rose again, we have an unshakeable hope for the future. He promised, "And if I go and prepare a place for you, I will come again, and receive you unto myself; that where I am, there ye may be also" (John 14:3).

Charles Spurgeon wrote, "Our divine Lord went to the undiscovered country, and He returned. He said that at the third day He would be back again, and He was true to His word. There is no doubt that there is another state for human life, for Jesus has been in it, and has come back from it. We have no doubt as to a future existence, for Jesus existed after death. We have no doubt as to a paradise of future bliss, for Jesus went to it and returned. His return from among the dead is a pledge to us of existence after death, and we rejoice in it."

One of the great needs people have today is hope. We live in a world groaning under the curse of sin. It is filled with hardship, death, pain, suffering, and evil. Our faith, based on the resurrection of Jesus Christ, does not insulate us from the suffering around us, but it does give us the wonderful and certain hope that God will triumph and that we will enjoy eternity in Heaven with Him. The Chrisitan who remembers Christ's resurrection can live a hope-filled life even during difficult circumstances.

—— Today's Renewal Principle ——

Rejoice in the hope that the resurrection gives us both for today and for eternity.

The Throne of Grace

Seeing then that we have a great high priest, that is passed into the heavens, Jesus the Son of God, let us hold fast our profession. For we have not an high priest which cannot be touched with the feeling of our infirmities; but was in all points tempted like as we are, yet without sin. Let us therefore come boldly unto the throne of grace, that we may obtain mercy, and find grace to help in time of need.—**Hebrews 4:14–16**

After the Children of Israel left Egypt for the Promised Land, God guided them to Mount Sinai where Moses received the Law from God. It was a fearsome place. If a person or animal touched the mountain, they were to be put to death. A fence was erected to keep people safe. "And it came to pass on the third day in the morning, that there were thunders and lightnings, and a thick cloud upon the mount, and the voice of the trumpet exceeding loud; so that all the people that was in the camp trembled" (Exodus 19:16).

The people needed a clear reminder of the holiness of God and His hatred of sin, and that is what they saw at Mount Sinai.

How different our experience with God is! The writer of Hebrews describes God having a "throne of grace." Rather than having a fence around it, the way into God's presence is open for us, and we can boldly come into His presence with the confidence that we have a right to be there. What changed? The difference is that Jesus paid the price for our sins and opened the way for us to freely come to God through His sacrifice.

A throne often symbolizes a place of judgment, but because of the grace that is freely offered us through salvation, God's throne becomes a place of comfort and help for us.

—— Today's Renewal Principle ——

The grace of God offers us the privilege of access to the very throne of Heaven. Avail yourself of that access through prayer.

A Renewal of Faith

And the apostles said unto the Lord, Increase our faith. And the Lord said, If ye had faith as a grain of mustard seed, ye might say unto this sycamine tree, Be thou plucked up by the root, and be thou planted in the sea; and it should obey you.—**Luke 17:5–6**

In many cases, Christ was quick to fulfill the disciples' requests. For instance, when they asked Jesus to teach them to pray, He did, giving them a pattern to follow. But when they asked Him to increase their faith, He did not. Instead, Jesus gave them an example of the miraculous things that could be accomplished with a tiny bit of faith— faith no bigger than a mustard seed. By the answer Christ gave, He pointed out that we do not so much need our faith increased, as we need it renewed. The problem we face is not primarily that our faith is too small, but that we do not use it enough.

The Christian life is a life of faith. We are saved by grace through faith, and we walk by faith not by sight (2 Corinthians 5:7). Simply put, faith is essential. "But without faith it is impossible to please him: for he that cometh to God must believe that he is, and that he is a rewarder of them that diligently seek him" (Hebrews 11:6). Our faith is based on the nature and character of God—He always keeps His promises—and it is a direct result of His Word. Romans 10:17 says, "So then faith cometh by hearing, and hearing by the word of God."

Each time we put our faith into action, even when it is not perfect or complete, we see God work, we are encouraged, and our faith is renewed.

Do you need a renewal of faith? Exercise your faith. Pray when the answer seems impossible. Witness when the heart seems hard. Give when the bank account is low. Rather than waiting until you have an amazing level of faith, act on the faith you already have.

—— Today's Renewal Principle ——

Strengthen and renew your faith today by putting it to work in your life.

Thirsting for God

As the hart panteth after the water brooks, so panteth my soul after thee, O God. My soul thirsteth for God, for the living God: when shall I come and appear before God?—**Psalm 42:1–2**

In 2001 an eighty-four-year-old man named Henry Morello was driving north of Phoenix, Arizona, when he realized he was heading the wrong direction. When he tried to turn around he got stuck in a ditch. Unable to walk to the main road to get help, he spent five days trapped in his car. To stay alive, he took a rock and cracked open the wiper fluid container in his car and drank the fluid. After he was rescued, doctors were amazed to find him in such good condition.

Those who are thirsty—truly thirsty—know what it is to seek something with a great desire. That level of desire should characterize our walk with God. We should seek Him above all others. He should be our greatest desire. God has promised that when we seek Him in this way, our search will be rewarded. In the Sermon on the Mount,

Jesus said, "Blessed are they which do hunger and thirst after righteousness: for they shall be filled" (Matthew 5:6).

Knowing how important it is for us to desire a close and intimate relationship with God, Satan offers us alternatives to satisfy our thirst apart from God. The first temptation in the Garden of Eden revolved around the promise that eating the fruit of the tree of the knowledge of good and evil would satisfy their need. Satan promised, "ye shall be as gods, knowing good and evil"(Genesis 3:5). Yet as with all of Satan's promises, this was a lie. There is no path to truth, love, beauty, and satisfaction apart from God. As we learn to reject the alternatives offered by the enemy, our thirst for God grows, and He will meet our needs.

—— **Today's Renewal Principle** ——

Do not allow anything else to quench the longing God has placed in your heart for Him—only He can satisfy.

Caring for the Broken Hearted

And there was delivered unto him the book of the prophet Esaias. And when he had opened the book, he found the place where it was written, The Spirit of the Lord is upon me, because he hath anointed me to preach the gospel to the poor; he hath sent me to heal the brokenhearted, to preach deliverance to the captives, and recovering of sight to the blind, to set at liberty them that are bruised, To preach the acceptable year of the Lord.
—**Luke 4:17–19**

When Cory Weissman, a student at Gettysburg College, took the floor for the final men's basketball game of the 2012 season, the crowd burst into applause. Cory, a star high school athlete, had suffered a massive stroke four years earlier. It had taken years of grueling physical therapy for him to be able to walk at all. He had no business on the court, but his coach wanted to reward his diligent effort in trying to recover from the stroke.

Cory limped his way up and down the court for a few minutes then went to the bench. With just a minute left and his team far ahead, the coach put Cory back in the lineup. The opposing coach instructed one of his players to foul Cory so that he would have a chance to score. After missing the first free throw, Cory shot again, scoring the only point of his college career. The Gettysburg assistant athletic director wrote saying that the opposing coach, "Displayed a measure of compassion that I have never witnessed in over thirty years of involvement in intercollegiate athletics."

Christians should be the most compassionate of all people, extending grace and hope to those who are hurting. This was the defining characteristic Jesus expressed at the beginning of His ministry, and it should describe us as well.

—— **Today's Renewal Principle** ——

The world is filled with hurting people. We can make a true difference in their lives if we reach out to them in compassion.

God's Way to the Top

Likewise, ye younger, submit yourselves unto the elder. Yea, all of you be subject one to another, and be clothed with humility: for God resisteth the proud, and giveth grace to the humble. Humble yourselves therefore under the mighty hand of God, that he may exalt you in due time: Casting all your care upon him; for he careth for you.—**1 Peter 5:5–7**

The great Bible teacher F. B. Meyer said, "I used to think that God's gifts were on shelves one above the other; and that the taller we grew in Christian character the easier we could reach them. I now find that God's gifts are on shelves one beneath the other; and that it is not a question of growing taller but of stooping lower; and that we have to go down, always down, to get His best gifts."

It is impossible for our finite minds to grasp the enormity of the gap between God and us. In our foolish pride, we often think that we have reached a high level in our spiritual walk or our intellectual knowledge, yet compared to God, we are less than nothing. God will never reward the proud, but He reaches down to those who are low in their own eyes and lifts them up. David is a wonderful example of this principle in action. He was content to tend his father's sheep, even after Samuel poured oil on his head and told him he would be king over Israel (1 Samuel 16:12, 13, 19).

David was in no hurry to place himself on the throne. In fact, when he twice was presented with the opportunity to kill Saul, he refused. He realized that the promotion that comes from God is much more meaningful and lasting than anything we can accomplish for ourselves. Rather than seeking approval and praise from men, we should seek to please God and leave the rest to Him.

—— Today's Renewal Principle ——

God is looking for people who are willing to trust Him enough to humble themselves so He can raise them up.

Crown Him Lord of All

The four and twenty elders fall down before him that sat on the throne, and worship him that liveth for ever and ever, and cast their crowns before the throne, saying, Thou art worthy, O Lord, to receive glory and honour and power: for thou hast created all things, and for thy pleasure they are and were created.—**Revelation 4:10–11**

Before a crucial battle during the Third Crusade, Phillip II of France came up with a unique means of motivating his soldiers. He took his royal crown off and placed it on a table, announcing that after the battle the crown would be given to the one who demonstrated the greatest courage and contributed the most to the victory. When the king had led his soldiers to a great triumph and the fighting ended, one of the nobles took the crown and placed it back on the king's head saying, "Thou, O king, art the most worthy."

One day when we see Jesus in Heaven, we will finally be able to fully comprehend the magnificent glory and majesty of our Saviour. Though we read of His glory in the Bible, our finite minds cannot truly understand His greatness. When we are in His presence, that will all be changed, and those who have served Jesus faithfully will be able to honor Him by returning to Him the trophies and crowns that He generously gives to us for our service.

He is high and lifted up, and our greatest glory in Heaven will be to join the host praising Jesus. Before the world was created the plan was in place for Jesus to come to Earth as our Saviour. His birth, life, death, and resurrection demonstrate the extent of God's love for us, and give us the hope of eternal life. One day all who know Him will unite to crown Him Lord of all.

—— Today's Renewal Principle ——

The crowns that we earn through service to God in this life are not for our benefit, but to cast at the feet of Jesus.

Avoiding the Truth

*For the time will come when they will not
endure sound doctrine; but after their own lusts
shall they heap to themselves teachers, having
itching ears; And they shall turn away their
ears from the truth, and shall be turned unto
fables.*—**2 Timothy 4:3–4**

The first martyr of the early church, Stephen,
was brought before the Sanhedrin for judgment
because of his powerful preaching about Jesus.
His sermon to the council, recorded in Acts 7, is
a masterpiece, weaving God's work in the history
of His chosen people with His plan of redemption.
His Spirit-filled message so convicted and enraged
those who heard it that they completely lost control.

Acts 7:54, 57 records, "When they heard these
things, they were cut to the heart, and they gnashed
on him with their teeth. Then they cried out with
a loud voice, and stopped their ears, and ran upon
him with one accord." They stoned Stephen to
death to avoid having to listen to the truth from
his lips. While they silenced Stephen, they could

not stop the truth. The church continued to grow as great numbers of people were saved, baptized, and added to it.

Our society has many people who clearly are not interested in listening to the truth. There are vast audiences for preachers who only say things the audiences want to hear. Yet the size and apparent success of such ministries does not equate to either their correctness or to God's blessing. He does not measure the effectiveness of our work by how many people agree with us but by how closely we adhere to His Word. It is critically important that we respond with a ready heart to the truth when it is presented to us. While it certainly is not comfortable to be corrected and reproved, it is far better than being allowed to continue on a path that leads to destruction.

——— Today's Renewal Principle ———

Rather than resisting the truth, we should be willing to heed correction and make necessary changes in our lives.

Making it Known

And when they had brought them, they set them before the council: and the high priest asked them, Saying, Did not we straitly command you that ye should not teach in this name? and, behold, ye have filled Jerusalem with your doctrine, and intend to bring this man's blood upon us.—**Acts 5:27–28**

Psychologist Dr. Robert Cialdini described an experiment he conducted on the campus of Arizona State University. During football season, he assigned researchers to count the number of students wearing anything that identified them with the team. They established a baseline number and then tracked what happened when the team won or lost. Following a victory, the number of students wearing team attire spiked, and following a loss, it went down dramatically. The public loyalty of the students was influenced by the performance of the team on the field.

God has called us to be public—committed and open—about our faith. Like the fans of a winning sports team, we should show our colors everywhere we go. The early church started with a handful of people, but in a short amount of time, their powerful preaching and consistent witnessing brought thousands to salvation and, as their enemies said, "filled Jerusalem." There was no question where they stood or where their allegiance was. They made it clear day after day, even in the face of opposition and persecution.

As culture moves further away from Christ, our willingness to take a public stand for Him becomes more important. We should never change our message to gain acceptance with the world. Instead we should stand with bold and firm convictions, clearly identified as believers. If every Christian would do that, we would see the world filled with the doctrines of Jesus Christ.

—— Today's Renewal Principle ——

Your life should make it clear to everyone who knows you that you are a follower of Jesus Christ.

Our Source of Joy

*And be not drunk with wine, wherein is excess; but
be filled with the Spirit; Speaking to yourselves in
psalms and hymns and spiritual songs, singing
and making melody in your heart to the Lord;
Giving thanks always for all things unto God
and the Father in the name of our Lord Jesus
Christ;*—**Ephesians 5:18–20**

Just before the Civil War, James Fields published
a poem called "The Captain's Daughter." In it,
he tells the story of a ship caught at sea during
a terrible winter storm. It is after midnight, but
everyone on board is too afraid to sleep. Finally
when all hope is gone, the captain goes below deck
and is ready to give up—until his daughter speaks:

> *But his little daughter whispered,*
> *As she took his icy hand,*
> *"Isn't God, upon the ocean,*
> *Just the same as on the land?"*

This reminder restored the faith of the captain,
and the following morning, they reached the

harbor safely. All of us go through experiences that are challenging—a serious health crisis, the loss of a job, a child who is struggling, or the death of a loved one. Bad things do happen to good people, even Christians. Some people respond to these difficulties with depression or anger at God for letting bad things happen to them. But others respond in faith and with a joy that remains in the midst of storms.

The difference in these responses is not found in the circumstances but in the degree to which the Holy Spirit is filling the hearts and lives of those believers. When we are full of Him, joy (a fruit of the Spirit) is a natural byproduct. We do not need everything to go well to be joyful. Instead, we need to have the Holy Spirit at work in our hearts.

—— Today's Renewal Principle ——

Regardless of your outward circumstances, your heart can be filled with joy through the filling of the Holy Spirit.

Even Now

Then Martha, as soon as she heard that Jesus was coming, went and met him: but Mary sat still in the house. Then said Martha unto Jesus, Lord, if thou hadst been here, my brother had not died. But I know, that even now, whatsoever thou wilt ask of God, God will give it thee.—**John 11:20–22**

Faith is not tested when things are going well; it is tested when things fall apart. In the moments of doubt, struggle, and loss, faith is put to the test. When Lazarus got sick, his sisters sent word to Jesus and asked for help, but He delayed coming until after Lazarus had died. When Jesus arrived, Martha expressed her faith in a definite and powerful way. She struggled in her trust, yet she did express that ultimately she knew Christ could do anything. Although her brother had been dead for four days she said, "even now" God could change that.

J. Vernon McGee said, "It makes less demand upon faith to believe that in a future day we shall receive glorified bodies than it does to rest now on the assurance that they that wait upon the Lord shall renew their strength. It is easier to believe that the Lord is coming and the dead will be raised than it is to believe that tomorrow I can live for God. It is so easy to comfort people who are mourning and say, 'Well, you'll see your loved ones someday.' That doesn't take much faith. It takes a lot of faith to say, 'I have just lost my loved one, but I am comforted with the assurance that God is with me and He does all things well.'"

When things don't work out the way we think they should, we are tempted to think that God has failed. Instead we should remember the "even now." No matter how hopeless things seem or how dark our circumstances, God is able to meet every need. He has our best interests at heart, and we can always trust Him.

—— **Today's Renewal Principle** ——
When your faith is tested, remember that God never fails to keep His promises.

The Beginning of the Fall

For the invisible things of him from the creation of the world are clearly seen, being understood by the things that are made, even his eternal power and Godhead; so that they are without excuse: Because that, when they knew God, they glorified him not as God, neither were thankful; but became vain in their imaginations, and their foolish heart was darkened. Professing themselves to be wise, they became fools,—**Romans 1:20–22**

In Romans 1, Paul describes the descent of a society that has turned away from God. Paul wrote in terms that could easily have been taken from the news headlines of our day. The culture he describes is the one in which we live. If we look back at the beginning of the process of decline and decay, we find a sin that leads directly to the downward path—not being thankful and failing to give God glory for what He has done. This is the first step on the road to folly and destruction.

Through Moses, God warned the children of Israel of this danger before they entered the land of Canaan. He told them that He would bless them with houses, vineyards, and orchards for which they would not have to work. This incredible economic blessing was coming to them solely because of God's gracious favor. Moses said that after they received all these good things, "Then beware lest thou forget the Lord, which brought thee forth out of the land of Egypt, from the house of bondage" (Deuteronomy 6:12).

When we are blessed with material things, we need to guard our hearts against the temptation to think that we have them because we deserve them, and instead give thanks to God for His grace. When we are not thankful, we place ourselves on the path to ruin. When we give God thanks, however, we will keep our hearts in a right relationship with Him.

—— Today's Renewal Principle ——
A failure of gratitude and praise will certainly lead to a failure of obedience.

The Power of Friendship

And it came to pass, when he had made an end of speaking unto Saul, that the soul of Jonathan was knit with the soul of David, and Jonathan loved him as his own soul. And Saul took him that day, and would let him go no more home to his father's house. Then Jonathan and David made a covenant, because he loved him as his own soul. —**1 Samuel 18:1–3**

Alfred Lord Tennyson was a famous poet who had numerous acquaintances but only a few true friends. His best friend was another poet, Arthur Hallam. Though Tennyson defeated Hallam in a poetry contest, they quickly became best friends, encouraging each other's work. Hallam used his connections and family money to encourage the publication of Tennyson's early poems, and later, Hallam was engaged to marry Tennyson's younger sister.

The death of Hallam at a young age deeply impacted Tennyson. Over the next seventeen years he worked on a poem about his friend that came to be known as "In Memoriam A. H. H." which contains these famous lines:

> *I hold it true, whate'er befall;*
> *I feel it when I sorrow most;*
> *'Tis better to have loved and lost*
> *Than never to have loved at all.*

A true friend is indeed a gift, encouraging us to dare and dream and do great things. We see this principle beautifully illustrated in the lives of David and Jonathan. Jonathan had every reason to hate David. The young shepherd boy who killed Goliath had the hearts of the people, and God had chosen him to rule in place of Saul, meaning Jonathan would never ascend to the throne. Yet rather than being resentful, Jonathan poured his heart into his friend, making his life better. This kind of friend is a gift from God.

—— **Today's Renewal Principle** ——

Resolve to be the kind of friend who makes the lives of others better rather than seeking the best for yourself.

Who Do You Serve?

Know ye not, that to whom ye yield yourselves servants to obey, his servants ye are to whom ye obey; whether of sin unto death, or of obedience unto righteousness? But God be thanked, that ye were the servants of sin, but ye have obeyed from the heart that form of doctrine which was delivered you. Being then made free from sin, ye became the servants of righteousness.—**Romans 6:16–18**

John Newton's gravestone reads "John Newton, Clerk, once an infidel and libertine, a servant of slaves in Africa, was by the rich mercy of our Lord and Saviour Jesus Christ, preserved, restored, pardoned, and appointed to preach the faith he had long labored to destroy." Most remember that Newton was a slave trader before his conversion, but many have forgotten that he was captured and served for a time as a slave himself in Africa. It was on his trip home to England after his rescue that Newton was saved.

All of us serve something or someone. We talk of being free, but everyone serves what they obey.

The choice is not *if* we will serve, but *who* (or what) we will serve. This is the challenge that Joshua posed to the Children of Israel near the end of his life: "And if it seem evil unto you to serve the Lord, choose you this day whom ye will serve; whether the gods which your fathers served that were on the other side of the flood, or the gods of the Amorites, in whose land ye dwell: but as for me and my house, we will serve the Lord" (Joshua 24:15).

The devil offers us freedom from God's yoke, but his lie conceals the heavier yoke he wants to place upon our shoulders. Jesus said, "For my yoke is easy, and my burden is light" (Matthew 11:30). Jesus did not say that there is no service in following Him, but that the way is easy instead of painful. It is a service that brings rest.

—— **Today's Renewal Principle** ——

Choosing to serve God is the only way to know and experience true freedom.

The Hope of Forgiveness

But he was wounded for our transgressions, he was bruised for our iniquities: the chastisement of our peace was upon him; and with his stripes we are healed. All we like sheep have gone astray; we have turned every one to his own way; and the LORD hath laid on him the iniquity of us all.—**Isaiah 53:5–6**

D.L. Moody told the story of a Scottish preacher who before his conversion had been a wicked man. Fighting and gambling made him well known in the community. After he was saved, he began preaching the gospel.

One night as he prepared to go to the pulpit in another town, someone handed him an envelope. Inside was a list of the awful things he had done in that town. He debated what to do for a moment, then stepped to the pulpit and began to speak: "Friends, I am accused of crimes and sins committed in this very city. I will read them to you." One after another he read these charges, and at the conclusion of each he said, "I am guilty."

When he had finished the whole list, he paused for a moment and then said, "You ask how I dare come to you and speak of righteousness and truth, with a list of crimes like that against my name? I will tell you: 'This is a faithful saying, and worthy of all acceptation, that Christ Jesus came into the world to save sinners; of whom I am chief' (1 Timothy 1 :15)."

On the cross, all of our sins were laid on Jesus Christ. He completely and forever paid the debt for all those who trust in Him for salvation. The amazing sacrifice of love that Christ made on the cross and the fulfillment of His promise of the resurrection give us the wonderful and certain hope of eternal life. Nothing in our past can take away this great gift.

—— Today's Renewal Principle ——

The past holds no power over the forgiven child of God and cannot rob us of our hope for the future.

A Renewal of Prayer

And it came to pass, that, as he was praying in a certain place, when he ceased, one of his disciples said unto him, Lord, teach us to pray, as John also taught his disciples. And he said unto them, When ye pray, say, Our Father which art in heaven, Hallowed be thy name. Thy kingdom come. Thy will be done, as in heaven, so in earth. Give us day by day our daily bread. And forgive us our sins; for we also forgive every one that is indebted to us. And lead us not into temptation; but deliver us from evil.—**Luke 11:1–4**

This is the only recorded place in Scripture where the disciples asked Jesus to teach them something. Though He was constantly teaching them as they went from place to place, the example the disciples saw in Jesus' prayer life moved them to ask Him for specific instruction on prayer: "Lord, teach us to pray." We must remember the central and vital importance of prayer to the successful Christian life.

In the Lord's Prayer, more accurately the model prayer, we see what Jesus thought was important in our prayers. We are to pray to honor and glorify the name of God. We should pray for His will to be done, both in our own lives and in the lives of others. We should pray daily for provision of our needs. We should ask forgiveness for our sins, and we should pray for deliverance from temptation. Every part and facet of life is a fit subject for prayer. If we do not pray, we miss the provision, protection, and victory God means for us to have.

William Cowper put it this way:

> *Restraining prayer, we cease to fight;*
> *Prayer makes the Christian's armor bright;*
> *And Satan trembles when he sees*
> *The weakest saint upon his knees.*

—— Today's Renewal Principle ——

If we have little prayer, we will have little power. If we have much prayer, we will have much power.

Faith to the Finish

*I thank my God upon every remembrance of you,
Always in every prayer of mine for you all making
request with joy, For your fellowship in the gospel
from the first day until now; Being confident
of this very thing, that he which hath begun a
good work in you will perform it until the day of
Jesus Christ:*—**Philippians 1:3–6**

Charles Spurgeon became a pastor when he
was just a teenager. One of the great resources
that encouraged him in the ministry was being
able to watch the life of another preacher—his
grandfather. That good man labored in the
same church for more than fifty years. Spurgeon
described this conversation from near the end of
his grandfather's life. "At the age of fourscore years,
he preached on still, until laden with infirmities,
but yet as joyful and as cheerful as in the heyday of
his youth, his time had come to die. He was able to
say truthfully, when last he spake to me, 'I do not
know that my testimony for God has ever altered,

as to the fundamental doctrines; I have grown in experience, but from the first day until now, I have had no new doctrines to teach my hearers.'"

The calling of God is not just for a few years of life; it is permanent. Romans 11:29 says, "For the gifts and calling of God are without repentance." God expects us to remain faithful to our marriages and families, to our churches and to His work all the days of our lives. While there may be others who quit the work or fall away, we can remain faithful, not because of our great strength or willpower, but because of the sustaining power of God. He has promised to finish the work He has begun in our lives. It is our obligation to remain at that work until He calls us home.

—— Today's Renewal Principle ——
Knowing that God is faithful and will uphold us should strengthen our commitment to remain faithful to Him to the end of our lives.

The Impact of Loving God

Hear, O Israel: The LORD our God is one LORD:
And thou shalt love the LORD thy God with all thine
heart, and with all thy soul, and with all thy might.
And these words, which I command thee this day,
shall be in thine heart:—**Deuteronomy 6:4–6**

If our walk with God is going to be what it should
be, it is imperative that we love God as we should.
Nothing else can be allowed to occupy the central
place in our thoughts, efforts, and emotions that
belongs to Him alone. Our love for God should
be so complete and all-encompassing that it
flows out in every word and action. Our love for
God should also cause us to live in harmony with
other Christians.

In a letter to the noted evangelist George
Whitefield, John Newton wrote, "The longer I live,
the more I see of the vanity and the sinfulness
of our unchristian disputes; they eat up the very
vitals of religion. I grieve to think of how often I
have lost my time and my temper in that way, in

presuming to regulate the vineyards of others, when I have neglected my own…. When our dear Lord questioned Peter, after his fall and recovery, he said not, 'Art thou wise, learned and eloquent?' nay, He said not, 'Art thou clear and sound, and orthodox?' But this only, 'Lovest thou me?'"

Our relationships are shaped by our love for God. When He is in His proper place on the throne of our hearts, everything else falls into alignment. Christians who love God as they should do not spend their time fighting over insignificant matters with others. Instead, like two instruments that have each been tuned properly, they act in harmony with each other. If we have trouble getting along with others, the underlying problem may be our lack of love for God.

—— Today's Renewal Principle ——

Our walk with other Christians is shaped by keeping our love for God strong.

How We View God

And to him they agreed: and when they
called the apostles, and beaten them, they
commanded that they should not speak in the
name of Jesus, and let them go. And they departed
from the presence of the council, rejoicing that
they were counted worthy to suffer shame for
his name. And daily in the temple, and in every
house, they ceased not to teach and preach
Jesus Christ.—**Acts 5:40–42**

Despite all of the persecution and opposition that they faced, the early church was characterized by being joyful. They had joy despite their circumstances because they were focused on Jesus. When they were beaten, they still had joy, because they saw it as evidence that they were viewed as worthy by the one who had given His life on the cross. Joy flows from our knowledge of God and a focus on His nature and character.

A.W. Tozer wrote, "What comes into our minds when we think about God is the most important thing about us. The history of mankind will probably show that no people has ever risen above its religion, and man's spiritual history will positively demonstrate that no religion has ever been greater than its idea of God. Worship is pure or base as the worshiper entertains high or low thoughts of God. For this reason the gravest question before the Church is always God Himself, and the most portentous fact about any man is not what he at a given time may say or do, but what he in his deep heart conceives God to be like."

The source of our joy is not the good things we enjoy or the pleasant circumstances we experience, but instead the God "who giveth us richly all things to enjoy" (1 Timothy 6:17). Being saved does not automatically make God the center of our thoughts and actions. That is a responsibility we must fulfill as His children.

—— Today's Renewal Principle ——

A Christian who is focused on who God is will not find a lack of reasons for joy.

A Love for Others

But when he saw the multitudes, he was moved with compassion on them, because they fainted, and were scattered abroad, as sheep having no shepherd. Then saith he unto his disciples, The harvest truly is plenteous, but the labourers are few; Pray ye therefore the Lord of the harvest, that he will send forth labourers into his harvest.
—**Matthew 9:36–38**

David Brainerd was orphaned as a teenager. A local pastor took him into his home. When he was twenty-one, Brainerd went to Yale as a student. He had been convinced that he could gain God's favor on his own, but he came under conviction during a revival and realized that salvation was only of God's grace. When Brainerd finished his education, he determined to be become a missionary to the American Indians. He declined the call to pastor a large and wealthy church in New York to live in poverty among the Indians.

He started works in Massachusetts, Pennsylvania, and New Jersey, traveling long miles and often sleeping outside in bad weather. Brainerd said, "I care not where I go or how I live or what I endure so that I may save souls." Never strong in body, Brainerd contracted pulmonary consumption and died in the home of Jonathan Edwards at the age of twenty-nine. Though he did not see as many converts as he hoped for during his lifetime, he did see hundreds of Native Americans trust Christ, and his story became a challenge that was used to call many to enter missionary work.

It is impossible for us to truly love God as we should without demonstrating a love for others. People we meet will spend eternity either in Heaven or Hell—and God has commanded us to tell them of the only hope of Heaven through salvation in Jesus Christ. There is no greater demonstration of God's love than sharing it with others.

—— Today's Renewal Principle ——

Your love for God is nowhere better seen than in your love for the lost.

Singing Grace

And let the peace of God rule in your hearts, to the which also ye are called in one body; and be ye thankful. Let the word of Christ dwell in you richly in all wisdom; teaching and admonishing one another in psalms and hymns and spiritual songs, singing with grace in your hearts to the Lord. And whatsoever ye do in word or deed, do all in the name of the Lord Jesus, giving thanks to God and the Father by him.—**Colossians 3:15–17**

It is not hard to keep a song in our hearts when things are going well. When the bills are paid and there is money in the bank, we sing. When we are healthy and the kids are doing well in school, we sing. When we are receiving quick answers to our prayers and the messages at church remind us of the visible blessings of God in our lives, we sing. But in God's plan, we are supposed to sing all the time, whether or not things are going the way we think they should. The only way we can do that is to have hearts that are filled with His grace.

One of the greatest New Testament churches was the church at Philippi. They were fervent in their evangelism and gave generously to support Paul as he traveled the world and preached the gospel, yet that church started in great difficulty and persecution. During Paul and Silas' first trip to Philippi, they were arrested, beaten, and thrown into jail for preaching the gospel. The beating was illegal under Roman law, but that did not keep the wounds from hurting.

Paul and Silas faced a choice. They could sulk (and they had reason to) or they could sing. "And at midnight Paul and Silas prayed, and sang praises unto God: and the prisoners heard them" (Acts 16:25). It was God's grace rather than their circumstances that had them singing even in the prison.

—— Today's Renewal Principle ——

To have a song of joy in difficult times, keep your heart focused on the grace of God.

Faith and Contentment

Not that I speak in respect of want: for I have learned, in whatsoever state I am, therewith to be content. I know both how to be abased, and I know how to abound: every where and in all things I am instructed both to be full and to be hungry, both to abound and to suffer need. I can do all things through Christ which strengtheneth me.—**Philippians 4:11–13**

Though the ministry of the Apostle Paul was greatly effective, it certainly was not easy. He was constantly being attacked for his preaching by the unbelieving Jewish leaders who opposed the message of Christ as the Messiah, by the pagan leaders who opposed the teaching against idolatry, and by the Roman authorities who viewed this new religion as a threat. Paul was beaten, jailed, stoned, shipwrecked, and had to flee for his life on multiple occasions. Yet throughout all the trials and challenges he faced, Paul's faith rested in Christ.

The church at Philippi started in the face of great persecution. One of the first members was the jailer who had been responsible for keeping Paul in the prison after his arrest until the earthquake freed him from his bonds. The letter we know as the book of Philippians was written by Paul while he was in jail in Rome for his fearless preaching. Despite all that he had endured and the trouble of his current surroundings, Paul could write that he was content.

True contentment has nothing to do with our possessions or our location; it has to do with our faith. Our God reminds us that both scarcity and abundance are according to His plan, and when we recognize that truth, we can find contentment in any situation. In turn, that contentment allows us to attempt great things for God, knowing that the strength given to us by Christ will be equal to any challenge we face.

——— Today's Renewal Principle ———

The more that we trust God's goodness and provision, the more content we are regardless of our circumstances.

The Fruit of Love

*But the fruit of the Spirit is love, joy, peace,
longsuffering, gentleness, goodness, faith,
Meekness, temperance: against such there is no
law.*—**Galatians 5:22–23**

Madalyn Murray O'Hair was successful in her
attempts to get Bible reading and prayer
removed from the public school system. Her group
American Atheists worked in states and cities across
the country to try to remove every trace of religion
from public life. But in 1995, O'Hair, her son, and
her granddaughter suddenly vanished. They were
later discovered to have been murdered by one of
the men who worked for her organization. After
O'Hair's death, her personal diaries were published.
Numerous times in the more than two thousand
pages she wrote, "Somebody somewhere, please
love me."

We live in a world that is starved for true,
genuine love. The substitutes our society offers
will never satisfy that longing. There are all kinds
of "love" around us, but it is not the kind of love

that is produced as a fruit of the Holy Spirit. When Christians are walking in the Spirit, love will be a natural by-product. The orange trees that grow in massive rows in the orchards of California do not have to be instructed to produce oranges; it is part of their nature. In the same way, love should be the defining characteristic of Christians.

When Mary and Martha sent word to Jesus that Lazarus was sick, He delayed coming until Lazarus was dead and had been buried for four days. Even though Jesus knew He was about to bring Lazarus back to life, His heart of compassion was still grieved at the sorrow of His friends, and He wept. Those who watched noticed that response. "Then said the Jews, Behold how he loved him!" (John 11:36). We are meant to treat others in such a way that our love for them is obvious.

—— Today's Renewal Principle ——

The only way to exhibit true godly love to everyone around us is for us to be filled with the Holy Spirit.

Describing God

For my thoughts are not your thoughts, neither are your ways my ways, saith the LORD. For as the heavens are higher than the earth, so are my ways higher than your ways, and my thoughts than your thoughts.—**Isaiah 55:8–9**

There is an ancient Indian story of six blind men trying to figure out what an elephant is like. Each of them touches a different part of the elephant, and as a result, they have very different impressions. One man touches the elephant's leg and says the elephant is like a strong column. Another touches the tail and says the elephant is like a rope. One touches the trunk and says the elephant is like a tree branch. One touches the ear and describes the elephant as being like a fan. Another touches the side of the elephant and says he is like a wall. The final man touches the tusk and says the elephant is like a pipe.

The reason they give such differing descriptions is that the elephant is much greater than they are capable of realizing without sight. In a far more significant way, God is so far beyond our understanding that it is impossible for us to fully comprehend or describe His nature. But the Bible gives us a simple description that sums up the essential part of His character: "God is love" (1 John 4:8).

Because love is so central to who God is, He expects love to be a central part of our lives as well: "Beloved, let us love one another: for love is of God; and every one that loveth is born of God, and knoweth God" (1 John 4:7). The more like God we become (as we walk in the Spirit day by day), the more love we will display toward others in our lives. As Jesus said, "By this shall all men know that ye are my disciples, if ye have love one to another" (John 13:35).

—— Today's Renewal Principle ——

If we are to truly live as children of God in deeds rather than just in title, we must live and walk in love.

Being an Approved Workman

Of these things put them in remembrance, charging them before the Lord that they strive not about words to no profit, but to the subverting of the hearers. Study to shew thyself approved unto God, a workman that needeth not to be ashamed, rightly dividing the word of truth. But shun profane and vain babblings: for they will increase unto more ungodliness.—**2 Timothy 2:14–16**

A.W. Tozer wrote, "Before the judgment seat of Christ my service will be judged not by how much I have done but by how much I could have done!…In God's sight, my giving is measured not by how much I have given but how much I have left after I made my gift….Not by its size is my gift judged, but by how much of me there is in it. No man gives at all until he has given all! No man gives anything acceptable to God until he has first given himself in love and sacrifice."

As Christians, we want to one day hear the words "Well done" from God. But being an approved workman is not a given. Only those who put forth the effort and sacrifice to do what they can and should do will receive this praise.

God gives us His grace and the power of the Holy Spirit to serve Him. None of us lacks, regardless of our level of talent or opportunity, what is necessary to be approved because God's approval is based on His measure of what we do with what we have. The widow who gave two mites gave far less than others, but she was the only one Jesus singled out for praise. It was her heart that made her gift grow into something far greater than it seemed and made her work approved (Luke 21:2–4).

So God gives us everything we need to serve Him, but He calls us to invest ourselves and to serve diligently from a pure heart.

—— Today's Renewal Principle ——

We should serve Christ every day in light of the reality that we will stand before Him and give account of our service.

The Anchor of Hope

Wherein God, willing more abundantly to shew unto the heirs of promise the immutability of his counsel, confirmed it by an oath: That by two immutable things, in which it was impossible for God to lie, we might have a strong consolation, who have fled for refuge to lay hold upon the hope set before us: Which hope we have as an anchor of the soul, both sure and stedfast, and which entereth into that within the veil;—**Hebrews 6:17–19**

Modern U.S. aircraft carriers are in many ways more like small towns than boats. With a crew of more than six thousand on board, they offer a full array of services—food, housing, medical, dental, hair cuts, exercise rooms, and more. Yet for all of the amenities, these powerful warships are still naval vessels, and, as ships have for centuries, they need anchors.

The anchors for an aircraft carrier are a far cry from the kind of anchors most boaters are familiar with. The anchor for an aircraft carrier weighs more than 60,000 pounds. In addition, each link in the anchor chain weighs more than 300 pounds. Taken together, the anchor and chain weigh over 700,000 pounds, and each aircraft carrier has two of them. Why? Because it is vitally important to have a source of stability when the storms come.

God's Word tells us that regardless of our circumstances we can hold fast to our hope for the future. This hope is based on the unchanging nature and integrity of God. Because He cannot lie, we can trust what He tells us. The Bible does not promise the absence of storms. Instead, it offers a means of keeping us safe when they come. As the great missionary Adoniram Judson said, "The future is as bright as the promises of God." Knowing God's love and care for us allows us to rejoice in hope no matter what happens.

—— **Today's Renewal Principle** ——

When the winds and storms are raging, allow your hope and trust in God's promises to keep you anchored and safe.

The Secret Place of Prayer

*And when thou prayest, thou shalt not be as the
hypocrites are: for they love to pray standing in
the synagogues and in the corners of the streets,
that they may be seen of men. Verily I say unto
you, They have their reward. But thou, when thou
prayest, enter into thy closet, and when thou hast
shut thy door, pray to thy Father which is in secret;
and thy Father which seeth in secret shall reward
thee openly.*—**Matthew 6:5–6**

Though there is certainly a place for public and
corporate prayer, and I have been in some
wonderful prayer meetings in my life, there is no
substitute for personal private petitions to our
Father in Heaven. The praying that we do in public
can never carry the depth of emotion and feeling
that our private prayers have. The Scottish pastor
Thomas Brooks said, "The power of religion and
godliness lives, thrives, or dies, as closet [private]
prayer lives, thrives, or dies. Godliness never rises
to a higher pitch than when men keep closest to
their closets."

Prayer—prevailing, powerful, Bible prayer—is a spiritual discipline. It requires an investment of time, energy, and emotion. A few words in a Sunday school class or a church service are no substitute for meaningful and personal time spent with God. We need to make prayer a habit just as Jesus did. Again and again in Scripture we read that He separated Himself from His disciples to spend time with His Father in prayer. Often, Jesus was extremely busy with the crowds pressing in to see Him and teaching and healing, so He began the day with prayer. "And in the morning, rising up a great while before day, he went out, and departed into a solitary place, and there prayed" (Mark 1:35). There is no more important priority that we have as believers than to spend time with God in prayer.

—— Today's Renewal Principle ——

If your life is marked by time spent alone with God in prayer, it will also be marked by His power.

Why Faith Pleases God

By faith Enoch was translated that he should not see death; and was not found, because God had translated him: for before his translation he had this testimony, that he pleased God. But without faith it is impossible to please him: for he that cometh to God must believe that he is, and that he is a rewarder of them that diligently seek him.
—Hebrews 11:5–6

Enoch makes a brief appearance on the pages of Scripture, but his story holds an important lesson regarding the role of faith in our lives. The one thing that stood out most in life, the central focus of his testimony, was that Enoch pleased God. There are many good things that could be said about a person, but I cannot think of a better one. From the time of his son's birth, Enoch walked with God in a close and special way. "And Enoch walked with God after he begat Methuselah *three hundred years, and begat sons and daughters*" (Genesis 5:22).

The writer of Hebrews, in the context of Enoch's life, tells us that without faith we cannot please God.

There are two parts to this equation. First, without faith, we have no desire for the close fellowship and relationship with God that Enoch had. We will not go to God on a regular basis if we do not have faith. God has chosen to reveal Himself to us primarily through the pages of Scripture. If we are looking for tangible, physical evidence we are looking in the wrong place. Faith sees the invisible.

Second, without faith, we will not pray. Prayer is the means through which God has ordained to meet our needs. Yet if we do not believe that He will hear and answer, why would we pray? Without faith, prayer withers. Without prayer, our spiritual walk and work wither.

—— Today's Renewal Principle ——

Since our Christian walk is only possible through faith, our lives should be steeped in the Word so our faith will grow and God will be pleased.

The Attraction of Love

Jesus answered and said, This voice came not because of me, but for your sakes. Now is the judgment of this world: now shall the prince of this world be cast out. And I, if I be lifted up from the earth, will draw all men unto me. This he said, signifying what death he should die.
–John 12:30–33

In his book *A Search for Souls*, Dr. L. R. Scarborough wrote, "Mr. Moody tells of a little street urchin in Chicago who went many, many blocks across the frozen streets of the great city, passing church and Sunday school after church and Sunday school, to the church served by Mr. Moody. A Sunday school teacher stopped him one morning and said, 'Where are you going?' He said, 'To Mr. Moody's Sunday school.' He said, 'Why, that is many, many blocks away. Come into my class in this Sunday school nearby.' The boy said, 'No.' The teacher persisted and finally asked the boy why he went so far through the cold across the city to Mr. Moody's Sunday school. He said, 'Because they love a fellow over there!' Lost souls are looking for love; they are longing for love; and if they find it not in our hearts and the atmosphere we create in our churches and Sunday schools, then they will go limping down to Hell without it!"

The scribes and Pharisees criticized Jesus because He ate with publicans, spoke to immoral women, and even touched lepers. These contacts were shocking to those who prided themselves on outward uprightness and wanted nothing to do with "sinners." Jesus, however, emphasized the priority of the heart and demonstrated love to those He met. As a result, "The common people heard him gladly" (Mark 12:37). His sacrificial love attracted people to Him. If we desire to reach people with Christ's love, we must likewise love them ourselves.

—— Today's Renewal Principle ——

When we treat those we meet with love and compassion, they will be drawn to the Saviour through our lives.

Leaving the Past Behind

Blessed is he whose transgression is forgiven, whose sin is covered. Blessed is the man unto whom the LORD imputeth not iniquity, and in whose spirit there is no guile.—**Psalm 32:1–2**

He was a ruthless killer. He did not just fly off in rage and kill. Instead he carefully planned his attacks, even travelling great distances to reach his victims. And he made a special point of targeting those who were followers of Christ. He was Saul of Tarsus, better known to us as the Apostle Paul.

Later in his life he would write, "And I thank Christ Jesus our Lord, who hath enabled me, for that he counted me faithful, putting me into the ministry; Who was before a blasphemer, and a persecutor, and injurious: but I obtained mercy, because I did it ignorantly in unbelief" (1 Timothy 1:12–13).

If Paul had allowed himself to carry continual guilt for what he had done before his salvation, he would have been unable to serve God in the effective way that he did. He was not bound by the chains of the past because he was confident in the forgiveness of Christ.

Many people live in bondage to sin that they have confessed to the Lord and that He has already forgiven. The devil torments them with reminders of how they failed God, yet God does not treat us that way. Sins that are forgiven are completely removed from the record.

Paul wrote one of the most powerful statements of this truth: "There is therefore now no condemnation to them which are in Christ Jesus, who walk not after the flesh, but after the Spirit" (Romans 8:1). If you are feeling condemned for a sin of which you have repented, that condemnation is not of God, and you have no reason for guilt. Rather, you can rest assured in the real and complete forgiveness of Christ.

—— Today's Renewal Principle ——

When our relationship with God is the source of our joy we will always have a reason to rejoice.

Born a King

Now when Jesus was born in Bethlehem of Judaea in the days of Herod the king, behold, there came wise men from the east to Jerusalem, Saying, Where is he that is born King of the Jews? for we have seen his star in the east, and are come to worship him. When Herod the king had heard these things, he was troubled, and all Jerusalem with him.—**Matthew 2:1–3**

When the wise men arrived in Jerusalem looking for Jesus, they turned the town upside down. Though Herod had been installed by the Romans, he was not popular with the majority of the people. His erratic and cruel behavior kept people constantly on edge in fear of their lives. News that there might be a potential rival to the hated ruler was certain to start a firestorm of rumors and gossip.

Yet in the midst of that chaos, there is a striking statement from the wise men. They asked for the one "born King of the Jews." The normal expression or title for the child who is born as heir to a throne is not a king, but a prince. From the very moment of His birth, Jesus was already King. He was, is, and always will be King, for God exists outside of time. Revelation 17:14 says, "These shall make war with the Lamb, and the Lamb shall overcome them: for he is Lord of lords, and King of kings: and they that are with him are called, and chosen, and faithful."

Our world today is badly in need of a renewed appreciation for who Jesus is. He is not merely a good man or a teacher who came to leave us an example to follow. Jesus is the Lord and King, and we must go to Him on His terms, or we do not go to Him at all.

—— Today's Renewal Principle ——

We should worship Jesus Christ as the rightful King of Heaven and Earth every day.

Showing Kindness

And the king said, Is there not yet any of the house of Saul, that I may shew the kindness of God unto him? And Ziba said unto the king, Jonathan hath yet a son, which is lame on his feet. And the king said unto him, Where is he? And Ziba said unto the king, Behold, he is in the house of Machir, the son of Ammiel, in Lodebar. Then king David sent, and fetched him out of the house of Machir, the son of Ammiel, from Lodebar.—**2 Samuel 9:3–5**

When Raymond Dunn was born in 1975, doctors thought he would only live a few days. Born with severe physical defects, Dunn could not speak or see. He did not grow normally, and as a teenager, he weighed less than forty pounds. But his family's determined love and care kept him alive. One of the biggest obstacles was finding something Dunn could eat. He was allergic to almost all foods except for a special Gerber baby food known as MBF. The problem was that with little demand for the product, Gerber discontinued it in 1985.

The family bought up all they could from around the country, but eventually the supply began to dwindle. After Dunn's mother made a desperate appeal, Gerber employees volunteered their time, and the company donated the materials and allowed the machines to be set up for a special run. Every two years for the rest of Raymond's life, the company would fire up the production line to turn out a new supply of MBF for the "Gerber Boy" as he came to be called. "It seemed like the right thing to do," said Dr. Sandra Bartholmey, a Gerber nutritionist. Raymond Dunn lived to be almost twenty years old because of kindness shown to him and his family.

If you look around today, you will easily find people who are desperate for a kind and encouraging word. Give it to them.

—— Today's Renewal Principle ——

When we treat people with kindness, we often open doors for them to receive a witness of the gospel.

The Test of Faith

*And it came to pass after these things, that
God did tempt Abraham, and said unto him,
Abraham: and he said, Behold, here I am. And
he said, Take now thy son, thine only son Isaac,
whom thou lovest, and get thee into the land of
Moriah; and offer him there for a burnt offering
upon one of the mountains which I will tell thee of.*
—Genesis 22:1–2

In June of 1859, a French acrobat and circus
performer named Jean-François Gravelet, better
known by his stage name of Charles Blondin,
astonished a great crowd of people by walking
across Niagara Falls on a tightrope. Blondin
had begun his performing career when he was
just a child, but this daring stunt made him a
household name. Thousands gathered to witness
this remarkable performance in the following days
as Blondin crossed and recrossed the dangerous
waters. He performed a number of unusual stunts
during his walks, including taking a small oven in
a wheelbarrow and cooking an omelet while on

the tightrope. Perhaps the single most amazing of Blondin's feats was carrying his manager, Harry Colcord, across the falls on his back.

It is likely that after Blondin had succeeded in crossing the falls several times that anyone in the crowd would have said they believed that he could do it again. But it took an incredible level of trust on the part of his manager to place his life on Blondin's back and allow himself to be carried across on that dangerous journey. That is real faith. It not only says that it believes, but it acts on what it believes.

It is easy to proclaim faith in the light. It is much harder to demonstrate faith in the darkness. Yet, in the dark moments when the struggles are real and the answer is unclear, we find out whether or not our faith is real.

—— Today's Renewal Principle ——

The only way to pass the test of your faith is to act on what God has said, no matter how difficult it may be.

Hope in God's Work

And he said unto me, My grace is sufficient for thee: for my strength is made perfect in weakness. Most gladly therefore will I rather glory in my infirmities, that the power of Christ may rest upon me. Therefore I take pleasure in infirmities, in reproaches, in necessities, in persecutions, in distresses for Christ's sake: for when I am weak, then am I strong.—**2 Corinthians 12:9–10**

We tend to think of the Apostle Paul as a giant of the faith because of all that he accomplished in his work for the Lord. While that is true, it is only part of the story. There are many times when Paul preached with little noticeable results, or when the only result was an attempt to kill him. Some of the churches that God used him to establish, like the church at Corinth, had serious problems. Some of his coworkers abandoned him when things got tough, like John Mark and Demas. Paul's success in his work for God was not because he never failed. He was a success because he never quit.

Whether he was seeing people come to Christ or fleeing town ahead of the people trying to kill him, Paul had confidence in his hope that God would bless the work. When things looked abysmal, he rejoiced because he knew that God's power could be better demonstrated then. Paul wrote, "Therefore, my beloved brethren, be ye stedfast, unmoveable, always abounding in the work of the Lord, forasmuch as ye know that your labour is not in vain in the Lord" (1 Corinthians 15:58).

If we lose the hope of the harvest, we may fail to see its fruit. Our faith in the promises of God enables us to maintain our hope even when things seem to be at their worst. We can rely on His faithfulness to ensure that His Word will always produce a result if we do not faint.

—— Today's Renewal Principle ——

Even if you do not see results immediately, never lose hope that God will provide the harvest He has promised.

How Love Forgives

And the son said unto him, Father, I have sinned against heaven, and in thy sight, and am no more worthy to be called thy son. But the father said to his servants, Bring forth the best robe, and put it on him; and put a ring on his hand, and shoes on his feet: And bring hither the fatted calf, and kill it; and let us eat, and be merry: For this my son was dead, and is alive again; he was lost, and is found. And they began to be merry.—**Luke 15:21–24**

Though there are many lessons that can be drawn from the story of the Prodigal Son, the main reason Jesus told the series of three parables that includes the well-known story of a father whose son left home and disgraced him was to highlight the error of the Pharisees. They were complaining because Jesus showed grace to the lost: "And the Pharisees and scribes murmured, saying, This man receiveth sinners, and eateth with them" (Luke 15:2). They wanted condemnation for the sinners, not realizing that they were just as much in need of God's grace and forgiveness.

When the younger son in Jesus' story returned home, having wasted all of his inheritance, his father greeted him with open arms. He did not rehash all of his son's sins and demand an accounting for them. He did not ask for his money to be returned with interest. He did not insist on a waiting period to prove that his son's repentance was real. He opened his arms and welcomed his son back into full fellowship with the family.

This is the way that God forgives us, and it is the pattern we should follow with others. God declares, "For I will be merciful to their unrighteousness, and their sins and their iniquities will I remember no more" (Hebrews 8:12). This kind of forgiveness prevents bitterness from growing in our hearts and destroying relationships.

—— Today's Renewal Principle ——

When true love forgives someone, it never holds the offense over his head again.

How Sin Hinders Prayer

Behold, the LORD'S hand is not shortened, that it cannot save; neither his ear heavy, that it cannot hear: But your iniquities have separated between you and your God, and your sins have hid his face from you, that he will not hear. For your hands are defiled with blood, and your fingers with iniquity; your lips have spoken lies, your tongue hath muttered perverseness.—**Isaiah 59:1–3**

In Samuel Taylor Coleridge's epic poem "The Rime of the Ancient Mariner," a ship becomes stranded in the open water when the wind stops blowing. One of those on board, the ancient mariner of the title, killed an albatross which led to the disaster. When the sailor tried to pray for help, he found his crime of killing the innocent bird blocking even his ability to pray. He recounted:

> *I looked to Heaven, and tried to pray*
> *But or ever a prayer had gusht,*
> *A wicked whisper came, and made*
> *My heart as dry as dust.*

Taylor touched on a truth found in Scripture: when we have unconfessed sin in our lives, prayer is nothing more than an empty religious ritual. Before we can expect God to work on our behalf, we must deal with the sins that keep Him from responding to our prayers. The notion that we can live any way we want and expect God to bail us out of whatever goes wrong is not based on Scripture. Samson tried this approach while he was a judge of Israel, but he found disaster on the path of sin.

The sins that we may hide from the world are certainly not hidden from God, and they not only hinder our prayers but keep us from enjoying the relationship with our Father that we should. Sin does not take us out of God's family, but it does take us out of the place of blessing. If there is sin, confession is the only prayer that will be effective.

—— Today's Renewal Principle ——

Before we expect an answer to our prayers, we should make sure that there is nothing in our lives hindering them.

The Hope of Transformation

Behold, what manner of love the Father hath bestowed upon us, that we should be called the sons of God: therefore the world knoweth us not, because it knew him not. Beloved, now are we the sons of God, and it doth not yet appear what we shall be: but we know that, when he shall appear, we shall be like him; for we shall see him as he is. And every man that hath this hope in him purifieth himself, even as he is pure.—**1 John 3:1–3**

Once when the noted preacher Dr. Harry Ironside was speaking in San Francisco, an agnostic businessman challenged him to a debate on the existence of God and the truth of the gospel. The businessman offered to pay all of the expenses and rent a building where they would each present evidence for their position. Ironside agreed to come on the condition that the agnostic would bring one man and one woman who had both fallen into some type of vice that had caused them to experience great loss and cost them favor within society, but who were now restored because of the positive changes and transformation caused by their new-found belief in agnosticism. Ironside said he could bring one hundred Christians who had been so transformed for every one the agnostic could find, and at that point the agnostic conceded.

The transformation that we experience at salvation is amazing, but it is only the beginning. The old nature is replaced with the new nature, and the process of sanctification begins. As we follow God's plan, we become more like Jesus. Romans 8:29 says, "For whom he did foreknow, he also did predestinate to be conformed to the image of his Son, that he might be the firstborn among many brethren." That process will not be complete until the day we see Jesus, but it should be continuing day by day as we wait for His return.

—— Today's Renewal Principle ——
The certain hope of Christ's return gives us a great motivation to purify our lives.

Courage to Share the Gospel

And now, Lord, behold their threatenings: and grant unto thy servants, that with all boldness they may speak thy word, By stretching forth thine hand to heal; and that signs and wonders may be done by the name of thy holy child Jesus. And when they had prayed, the place was shaken where they were assembled together; and they were all filled with the Holy Ghost, and they spake the word of God with boldness.—**Acts 4:29–31**

A fter both of his sons enlisted in the Army to fight in World War II, Henry Gerecke, the pastor of a small church in Missouri, volunteered to join the Army as a chaplain. In addition to his skill with the Word of God, Gerecke spoke fluent German. He was often called on to work with German prisoners as the Army moved forward. When the war ended, the Army asked him to serve as chaplain to the members of the German high command facing trial at Nuremberg.

Some people opposed the idea, believing that war criminals like Herman Goering and

Alfred Jodl did not deserve spiritual comfort. But Gerecke answered the call, even though doing so meant another year away from his wife and home. Eleven of the twenty-one tried at Nuremberg were sentenced to death. Gerecke continued to witness and minister to them up to the day of execution. He later wrote that four of them "died as penitent sinners trusting God's mercy for forgiveness. They believed in Jesus who shed His blood for their sins."

Most of us do not face the challenge of sharing the gospel with hardened criminals who have the blood of multiplied thousands on their hands. Yet, in truth, every sinner, whether his sins are small or great in our eyes, stands condemned to death and eternity in Hell apart from God's grace. Let us never fail to witness to anyone because of fear.

—— Today's Renewal Principle ——

There are no people whose sins are so severe that the grace of God cannot save them, so we should witness boldly to all.

Work and Prayer Together

For the builders, every one had his sword girded by his side, and so builded. And he that sounded the trumpet was by me. And I said unto the nobles, and to the rulers, and to the rest of the people, The work is great and large, and we are separated upon the wall, one far from another. In what place therefore ye hear the sound of the trumpet, resort ye thither unto us: our God shall fight for us.—**Nehemiah 4:18–20**

I read a story about one of D. L. Moody's trips across the Atlantic to preach. During the voyage, a great danger arose as a fire started below decks on the ship. There were not enough members of the crew to make a chain to pass buckets of water below, so they were joined by the passengers to fight the fire. One of those traveling with Moody suggested that they go away from the commotion and pray. Moody replied, "Not so, sir; we stand right here and pass buckets and pray hard all the time." Moody often said, "Prayer and work are the two hands of one person, and they should never be separated."

Prayer is vitally important, but it is no substitute for doing what we are able to do. When Nehemiah was leading the people in the work to rebuild the walls of Jerusalem, they faced great opposition. The threats were so dire that they carried their weapons with them to the walls while they worked. They prayed often and prayed much, but that did not substitute for their time spent at work. God could have arranged things so that we wake up every morning with all of our work completed and all of our needs met, but He knows that we need the disciplines of work and prayer. So He offers us His help and power while expecting us to do our part.

—— Today's Renewal Principle ——

The challenges that we face are best addressed by a combination of both prayer and hard work.

Faith and Unbelief

And ofttimes it hath cast him into the fire, and into the waters, to destroy him: but if thou canst do any thing, have compassion on us, and help us. Jesus said unto him, If thou canst believe, all things are possible to him that believeth. And straightway the father of the child cried out, and said with tears, Lord, I believe; help thou mine unbelief.—**Mark 9:22–24**

African impalas have powerful legs, so powerful that they can leap to a height of over ten feet and cover more than thirty feet in a single bound. Because of this amazing ability, you would think that a very large fence would be necessary when they are kept in a zoo. Yet, in fact, a fence only a few feet high will keep them safely contained as long as they cannot see what is on the other side of the fence. The impala will not jump if he cannot see where he will land.

Sometimes we are like the impala in that we are only willing to exercise our "faith" if we are pretty sure of the outcome. But true faith is not based on what we can see. Many times we are held in captivity by the fears of life when, if we would only trust God, we could live in the freedom He provides.

While Jesus was on the Mount of Transfiguration, a distraught father brought his demon possessed son to the disciples. He begged the disciples to cast out the demon, but they were unable to do so. When Jesus returned, the father went to Him for help. Jesus told him that his son could be free "If thou canst believe." In response, the father revealed a common problem that many of us have faced, he had both faith and doubt. In his desperation, he expressed his faith and asked Jesus for help with his doubts. Jesus responded by casting out the demon and restoring his son. When we act on the faith we have, God works.

—— Today's Renewal Principle ——

Listen to your faith instead of your fears, and you will find that your faith grows and your fears diminish.

The Real Work of the Church

And when he was come into the ship, he that had been possessed with the devil prayed him that he might be with him. Howbeit Jesus suffered him not, but saith unto him, Go home to thy friends, and tell them how great things the Lord hath done for thee, and hath had compassion on thee. And he departed, and began to publish in Decapolis how great things Jesus had done for him: and all men did marvel.—**Mark 5:18–20**

People who came in contact with Jesus had their lives dramatically transformed. One of the most remarkable transformations was seen in the life of the maniac of Gadera. This demon-possessed man had been driven out of town and was living among the tombs. The demons gave him inhuman strength so that he could not be bound. Yet, after Jesus cast out the demons, the people of the town found him, "sitting, and clothed, and in his right mind" (Mark 5:15).

He expressed a desire to join the followers of Jesus and travel with Him, but Jesus gave him a mission: go back to those who had known him before and give witness to the transformation that God's grace had brought about in his life. Oswald Smith said, "Oh, my friends, we are loaded down with countless church activities, while the real work of the church, that of evangelizing the world and winning the lost, is almost entirely neglected."

I am delighted to be a part of a church where there is a lot going on. There is a spirit of life and activity around our church that offers people a variety of ways to fellowship, learn, share, and grow. But, while there are many things that are good and helpful, the most important activity of the church is our soulwinning efforts. That is the command of Christ for the church. If that is lost, no program can substitute for it.

—— Today's Renewal Principle ——

There is nothing we can do with our lives that is more important than bringing others to faith in Christ.

The Worship of Heaven

And I looked, and, lo, a Lamb stood on the mount Sion, and with him an hundred forty and four thousand, having his Father's name written in their foreheads. And I heard a voice from heaven, as the voice of many waters, and as the voice of a great thunder: and I heard the voice of harpers harping with their harps: And they sung as it were a new song before the throne, and before the four beasts, and the elders: and no man could learn that song but the hundred and forty and four thousand, which were redeemed from the earth.
—**Revelation 14:1–3**

There are so many wonderful things about Heaven that all of the books in the world could not contain them, and even if they were written down, our finite minds could not grasp the infinite wonder that awaits us in eternity. But the great glory of Heaven is not a golden street, or gates carved from pearls, or even foundations made of precious stones. It is the wonderful presence of the Son of God.

Charles Spurgeon said, "Beloved, if we were allowed to look within the vail which parts us from the world of spirits, we should see, first of all, the person of our Lord Jesus. If now we could go where the immortal spirits day without night circle the throne rejoicing, we should see each of them with their faces turned in one direction; and if we should step up to one of the blessed spirits, and say, 'O bright immortal, why are thine eyes fixed? What is it that absorbs thee quite, and wraps thee up in vision?' He, without deigning to give an answer, would simply point to the centre of the sacred circle, and lo, we should see a Lamb in the midst of the throne. They have not yet ceased to admire His beauty, and marvel at His wonders and adore His person."

—— Today's Renewal Principle ——

Since we are going to spend eternity worshiping Jesus, it is a good idea to start practicing now.

A Pattern of Praise

I will bless the LORD at all times: his praise shall continually be in my mouth. My soul shall make her boast in the LORD: the humble shall hear thereof, and be glad. O magnify the LORD with me, and let us exalt his name together. I sought the LORD, and he heard me, and delivered me from all my fears.—**Psalm 34:1–4**

In December of 1920, Vice President-elect Calvin Coolidge (then governor of Massachusetts) went to Plymouth Rock to celebrate the three hundredth anniversary of the Pilgrims' landing in the New World. In his remarks, he highlighted the vital role that faith played in their lives: "There was among them small trace of the vanities of life. They came undecked with orders of nobility. They were not children of fortune but of tribulation. Persecution, not preference, brought them hither; but it was a persecution in which they found a stern satisfaction. They cared little for titles; still less for the goods of this earth; but for an idea they would die. Measured by the standards of men of their time, they were the humble of the earth. Measured by later accomplishments, they were the mighty. In appearance weak and persecuted they came—rejected, despised—an insignificant band; in reality strong and independent, a mighty host of whom the world was not worthy, destined to free mankind."

The Pilgrims were routinely thankful, not just when things were going well and all their needs were being met. We remember the Thanksgiving celebration they had after a great harvest, but they were also thankful during the harsh winter prior when there was little to eat and many died.

We are meant to praise God, not just in bits and spurts when life looks good, but day after day and throughout the day, we should fill both our hearts and our mouths with praise to God.

—— Today's Renewal Principle ——

The Lord's goodness and faithfulness is consistent day after day, and our praise to Him should be as well.

Joy from Mourning

The Spirit of the Lord GOD is upon me; because the LORD hath anointed me to preach good tidings unto the meek; he hath sent me to bind up the brokenhearted, to proclaim liberty to the captives, and the opening of the prison to them that are bound; To proclaim the acceptable year of the LORD, and the day of vengeance of our God; to comfort all that mourn; To appoint unto them that mourn in Zion, to give unto them beauty for ashes, the oil of joy for mourning, the garment of praise for the spirit of heaviness; that they might be called trees of righteousness, the planting of the LORD, that he might be glorified.—**Isaiah 61:1–3**

When Dr. Lee Roberson experienced the death of his baby daughter, the brokenhearted pastor and his wife did not understand the purpose of God, but they knew that He was always faithful. Out of that tragedy, the Robersons founded a camp for children where for decades thousands of children attended free of charge and heard the gospel. Rather than giving up on God,

Dr. Roberson found a way to help others through his pain.

Dr. Roberson said, "The Lord never fails. We do, but He cannot. The world fails, but He cannot. By faith you keep going forward. By faith attempt great things for God. When we lost our baby Joy, God led me to start Camp Joy for children. God supplied the property and the money. Rejoice in your darkest hour. The world may think you crazy, foolish; but keep trusting God, keep building your faith on the Word of God. Rest in that Book. Do what He says to. He will help you, lead you in the same way He led Moses, Elijah, Jeremiah, David, Peter, James and John, and the Apostle Paul."

Are you going through a time of sorrow? Remember God's promise: "Weeping may endure for a night, but joy cometh in the morning" (Psalm 30:5).

—— Today's Renewal Principle ——

Look for God's plan in your sorrow, and He will show you unexpected joy.

Day
54

Compassion Makes a Difference

Mine eye runneth down with rivers of water for the destruction of the daughter of my people. Mine eye trickleth down, and ceaseth not, without any intermission, Till the LORD look down, and behold from heaven. Mine eye affecteth mine heart because of all the daughters of my city.
—**Lamentations 3:48–51**

I read about an elderly lady who frequently went to a particular post office branch in her town because the employees there were so friendly. One year, just before Christmas, she was standing in a long line to buy stamps. Another person standing in line struck up a conversation with her and found out why she was there. He reminded her that there was a stamp machine in the lobby that she could use to avoid the line. "I know," she replied, "but the machine won't ask me about my arthritis!"

People today have more ways to communicate and connect than ever before, but we live in a society filled with people who are lonely and desperately wanting someone to care about them. With billions of people on the planet, most have few true friends. The world has become increasingly process-and-progress-focused, and as a result, meaningful personal relationships are often lacking.

This longing for someone to genuinely care is an open door to caring Christians who are looking for opportunities to witness. Jude wrote, "And of some have compassion, making a difference" (Jude 1:22). When we look at the life of Christ, we see that His interactions with people were characterized by a genuine concern for their needs. At the grave of Lazarus, knowing that He was about to raise His friend from the dead, Jesus still wept for the sorrow and pain of the grieving family. The lost world around us needs to hear and see a message of compassion and hope.

—— Today's Renewal Principle ——

If you demonstrate genuine care and compassion for others, you will not lack for people to whom you can effectively witness.

Our Impact on Others

Let us hold fast the profession of our faith without wavering; (for he is faithful that promised;) And let us consider one another to provoke unto love and to good works: Not forsaking the assembling of ourselves together, as the manner of some is; but exhorting one another: and so much the more, as ye see the day approaching. —**Hebrews 10:23–25**

Attitudes are contagious. A griping, complaining, critical person is likely to soon be surrounded by others who share his sour outlook. On the other hand, a joyful, happy, encouraging person is going to be a positive influence on those he meets. While there are many reasons Christian fellowship is important, one of the greatest is the impact that we have on each other. The world is filled with discouraging voices. When we come together as a church or as a group of believers in fellowship, we have the opportunity to share our joy and increase our strength. This aspect of joy is vital. It is not just internal, but joy produces great external results as well.

One lady recounted a story from many years ago that illustrates this truth. She wrote: "I remember a day when I had an errand downtown. I caught a streetcar, which was pretty well filled. The seats were the long ones, so we all faced one another, as well as the weather. It was a damp, dismal day and I imagined everyone was going to work, but no one seemed happy about it. Then the miracle—a woman got on the car with a baby about a year old. A little blond baby all smiles and bounce and full of giggles, and do you know that baby put on a show! She clapped her hands with pattycake, laughed and bounced up and down and with that bit of sunshine no one could feel dismal. Soon everyone was laughing and joining the baby in happiness."

—— **Today's Renewal Principle** ——

Joy is not meant for ourselves alone. God desires to influence and encourage others through our cheerful attitude toward life.

Sacrificial Love

This is my commandment, That ye love one another, as I have loved you. Greater love hath no man than this, that a man lay down his life for his friends. Ye are my friends, if ye do whatsoever I command you.—**John 15:12–14**

Maria Dyer was born in 1837 on the mission field in China where her parents were pioneer missionaries. Both her parents died when Maria was a little girl, and she was sent back to England to be raised by an uncle. The loss of her parents, however, did not deter her young heart from the importance of sharing the gospel. At age sixteen, she, along with her sister, returned to China to work in a girl's school as missionaries themselves. Five years later, Maria married Hudson Taylor, a man remembered today for his ministry of faith and sacrifice.

Hudson and Maria's work was often criticized, even by other Christians. At one point Maria wrote, "As to the harsh judgings of the world, or the more painful misunderstandings of Christian brethren, I generally feel that the best plan is to go on with our work and leave God to vindicate our cause." Of their nine children, only four survived to adulthood. Maria herself died of cholera when she was just forty-three, but she believed the cause was worthy of the sacrifice. On her grave marker these words were inscribed: "To her to live was Christ, and to die was gain."

In a day when many are self-absorbed and care more about what they can get rather than what they can give, we need a renewal of sacrificial love. It was God's love for us that sent Jesus into the world to die for our sins, and it is that kind of giving love that our world needs so greatly today. When we love God as we should, our interests fade as we magnify Him.

—— Today's Renewal Principle ——

It is impossible to love God and others as we should without being willing to sacrifice for them.

Faith to Give

But this I say, He which soweth sparingly shall reap also sparingly; and he which soweth bountifully shall reap also bountifully. Every man according as he purposeth in his heart, so let him give; not grudgingly, or of necessity: for God loveth a cheerful giver. And God is able to make all grace abound toward you; that ye, always having all sufficiency in all things, may abound to every good work:—**2 Corinthians 9:6–8**

Paul Harvey, a widely popular radio host for many years, often included humorous true stories that illustrated human behavior: "The Butterball Turkey Company set up a telephone hotline to answer consumer questions about preparing holiday turkeys. One woman called to inquire about cooking a turkey that had been in the bottom of her freezer for twenty-three years. That's right—twenty-three years. The Butterball representative told her the turkey would probably be safe to eat if the freezer had been kept below zero for the entire twenty-three years. But the Butterball representative warned her that even if the turkey was safe to eat, the flavor would probably have deteriorated to such a degree that she would not recommend eating it. The caller replied, 'That's what I thought. We'll give the turkey to our church.'"

Though there are many reasons that people are reluctant to give their best to the Lord, many of them can be traced to a lack of faith. When we do not truly believe God's promises to provide for our needs, it is easy for us to fall into the trap of hoarding everything we have. Faith gives generously because it believes that the law of sowing and reaping will create a return on what is given that far outweighs what would come from keeping it.

—— Today's Renewal Principle ——

If you trust God to keep His promises, there is no reason not to give generously as He commands.

The Courage to Stand

For we wrestle not against flesh and blood, but against principalities, against powers, against the rulers of the darkness of this world, against spiritual wickedness in high places. Wherefore take unto you the whole armour of God, that ye may be able to withstand in the evil day, and having done all, to stand. Stand therefore, having your loins girt about with truth, and having on the breastplate of righteousness;—**Ephesians 6:12–14**

In the 1950s, a professor named Solomon Asch conducted a series of experiments to measure the influence of peer pressure on an individual. In the experiments, a group of college students were brought in and told that they were undergoing a perception exercise. After being shown a line, the students were asked to correctly match it to another line of the same length. All of the students except for one in each group had already been told what answer to give.

The test was designed so that the correct answer would be obvious. The true subject of the experiment would be seated last in the group so that everyone else would answer first. After a few trial runs during which everyone gave the correct answer, the real experiment would begin. On some questions, all of the other students would deliberately give the same wrong answer. In many cases, the test subject would go along with the group; in fact, 75 percent of the subjects gave at least one wrong answer during the tests.

There is enormous power in peer pressure, and often that pressure is put on us to go along with something which we know to be wrong. The truth is under assault in our day, and many people are abandoning it in order to be better accepted or to avoid being criticized or persecuted. What we need instead are Christians who have firm beliefs and convictions and will not be swayed by anyone.

—— Today's Renewal Principle ——

Even if no one else is willing to do what is right, we need the courage to stand firm.

Take the Grace Offered

Follow peace with all men, and holiness, without which no man shall see the Lord: Looking diligently lest any man fail of the grace of God; lest any root of bitterness springing up trouble you, and thereby many be defiled; Lest there be any fornicator, or profane person, as Esau, who for one morsel of meat sold his birthright.—**Hebrews 12:14–16**

A minister friend of D.L. Moody named Dr. Anton used a sermon illustration about a dog to powerfully demonstrate how we fail to take advantage of the grace God freely offers to us. He said, "You have been sometimes out at dinner with a friend, and you have seen the faithful household dog standing watching every mouthful his master takes. All the crumbs that fall on the floor he picks up and seems eager for them, but when his master takes a plate of beef and puts it on the floor and says, 'Rover, here's something for you,' he comes up and smells of it, looks at his master, and goes away to a corner of the room. He was willing to eat the crumbs, but he wouldn't touch the roast beef—thought it was too good for him."

He went on to say, "That is the way with a good many Christians. They are not willing to take all God wants. Come boldly to the throne of grace and get the help we need; there is an abundance for every man, woman and child in the assemblage."

While grace never fails, there are times when we do not allow it to produce its full impact on our lives. It is a tragedy when this happens because grace means so much in our lives. The writer of Hebrews warns us to be careful because there is a very real danger of destruction. We cannot live the Christian life apart from God's grace applied on a daily basis.

—— Today's Renewal Principle ——

The only way that grace can fail is if we fail to take advantage of what is offered to us.

Consistency in Prayer

Praying always with all prayer and supplication in the Spirit, and watching thereunto with all perseverance and supplication for all saints; And for me, that utterance may be given unto me, that I may open my mouth boldly, to make known the mystery of the gospel, For which I am an ambassador in bonds: that therein I may speak boldly, as I ought to speak.—**Ephesians 6:18–20**

When he was on his deathbed, the powerful preacher John Knox, who led the Scottish Reformation, asked his wife to get the Bible and read to him. He said, "Read me that Scripture where I first cast my anchor." She began reading from the prayer of Jesus in John 17. The old preacher gained new strength and began praying. He asked God to save those who were still lost. He asked for the growth of those who had recently been saved. He asked for the protection of those facing persecution for their faithful witness. While he was praying, Knox died and entered the presence of the One to whom he had just been speaking. It is little wonder that Queen Mary said, "I fear his prayers more than an army of ten thousand men."

The Christian life must be a life of prayer if it is to have any meaningful and lasting impact on the world. The prayerless Christian will be a powerless Christian. Prayer is not just for those in full time Christian service, but for every believer. It is not just for the young or the troubled. Prayer is intended to be a regular, continual, and consistent practice of the believer. Through prayer, we pour out our hearts to God and seek His help. Through prayer, we receive the things that we need both physically and spiritually. Through prayer, we touch both Heaven and Earth, and accomplish what is impossible without Divine help.

—— Today's Renewal Principle ——

Until we reach Heaven, there will never be a day when we do not urgently need to pray.

The Cost of Evangelism

They that sow in tears shall reap in joy. He that goeth forth and weepeth, bearing precious seed, shall doubtless come again with rejoicing, bringing his sheaves with him.—**Psalm 126:5–6**

There is great joy in Heaven and on Earth when someone trusts Christ as Saviour. Yet it is very often the case that the process of reaching someone with the gospel is long and painful. While there are people who are saved the first time they hear the Good News, sometimes lengthy periods of prayer, work, and conversation precede the decision to accept God's gift of grace. Frequently during those times, those who are witnessing find their hearts breaking. Yes, there is rejoicing when someone is saved, but that may be preceded by sorrow.

Charles Spurgeon said, "Reckon then that to acquire soulwinning power, you will have to go through mental torment and soul distress. You must go into the fire if you are going to pull others out of it, and you will have to dive into the floods if you are going to draw others out of the water." There are many times when the painful experiences of our lives are the very thing that opens the door for us to present the gospel to someone. It was no doubt painful to be beaten and thrown into jail in Philippi, but as a result, Paul and Silas saw the jailer and his whole family saved.

When we look at the task of reaching the lost, we need to do so with an appreciation for the cost that it may entail. This should not come as a surprise, for while salvation comes to us at no cost, it was purchased by Christ at great expense on the cross. Just as He was willing to pay the price for our salvation, we should be willing to pay the price to reach others with the gospel.

—— Today's Renewal Principle ——

If we are going to be effective soulwinners, we must be willing to pay the price and shed the tears. Rejoicing is sure to follow.

Serious Confession

*If we say that we have no sin, we deceive ourselves,
and the truth is not in us. If we confess our sins, he
is faithful and just to forgive us our sins, and to
cleanse us from all unrighteousness. If we say that
we have not sinned, we make him a liar, and his
word is not in us.*—**1 John 1:8–10**

I read about a man who responded to the
invitation at an evangelistic service. "I am a
Christian," he told the man who met him at the altar,
"but there is a sin in my life, and I need help." The
counselor read some verses of Scripture and then
encouraged him to confess his sins to God. The
man began to pray, "Oh, Father, if we have done
anything wrong—" The counselor interrupted him.
"Don't drag me into your sin! There is no 'if' or 'we'
involved. If you want forgiveness, you need to get
down to business with God!"

Often we try to minimize our sin. We blame
others rather than accepting the responsibility for
what we have done. We make excuses to downplay

and deflect our guilt. If we want to experience the forgiveness and restoration that God promises, we must genuinely confess. The Bible principle of confession is a full admission of responsibility and an agreement with God about the nature of our sin.

From the very first sin in the Garden of Eden, when Adam blamed Eve for eating the forbidden fruit, people have been attempting to avoid dealing with their sin. Because of God's holy hatred of sin, He is not interested in our excuses, and He will not accept our half-hearted apologies for what we barely admit having done. In his great song of repentance, David wrote, "The sacrifices of God are a broken spirit: a broken and a contrite heart, O God, thou wilt not despise" (Psalm 51:17).

—— Today's Renewal Principle ——

Treat your sin with the same seriousness that God does, and you will experience His restoration.

Don't Keep It to Yourself

And there was one Anna, a prophetess, the daughter of Phanuel, of the tribe of Aser: she was of a great age, and had lived with an husband seven years from her virginity; And she was a widow of about fourscore and four years, which departed not from the temple, but served God with fastings and prayers night and day. And she coming in that instant gave thanks likewise unto the Lord, and spake of him to all them that looked for redemption in Jerusalem.—**Luke 2:36–38**

When Mary and Joseph took the baby Jesus to Jerusalem for his dedication ceremony, they met a woman who had dedicated her life to the service of God. The first thing she did was give thanks to God for the fulfillment of His promise to send a Saviour for the world. Then she told everybody she could about Jesus! These two things go beautifully together. When we are filled with gratitude and praise for our salvation, we find it easy to share the Good News with others.

In the Old Testament there is a wonderful story from the days of the prophet Elisha. The city of Samaria was besieged by an enemy army. Four lepers who had been kept outside the city walls even with an enemy army camped nearby were the first to discover that God had worked a miracle to deliver His people from the enemy. They made their way to the camp of the Syrians and found it deserted. They helped themselves to the spoils and riches left behind but realized they had to share the news. "Then they said one to another, We do not well: this day is a day of good tidings, and we hold our peace" (2 Kings 7:9). If we are truly thankful for the gift of salvation, the natural response is for us to share the Good News with others.

—— Today's Renewal Principle ——

Reflect today on the blessing of your salvation, and look for someone who is not saved with whom you can share the gospel.

Standing Firm

And others had trial of cruel mockings and scourgings, yea, moreover of bonds and imprisonment: They were stoned, they were sawn asunder, were tempted, were slain with the sword: they wandered about in sheepskins and goatskins; being destitute, afflicted, tormented; (Of whom the world was not worthy:) they wandered in deserts, and in mountains, and in dens and caves of the earth.—**Hebrews 11:36–38**

Although Charles Spurgeon was a popular and respected preacher, when he took a stand against the liberal theology that was infecting the Baptist Union in England, he stood almost alone. Lifelong friends turned against him, accusing him of valuing truth over unity. In this heartbreaking experience, Spurgeon refused to compromise. At one point, he said, "I know of nothing which I would choose to have as the subject of my ambition for life than to be kept faithful to my God till death, still to be a soul winner, still to be a true herald of the cross, and testify the name of Jesus to the last hour."

Loving and serving God does not guarantee short term success. Jesus said, "If ye were of the world, the world would love his own: but because ye are not of the world, but I have chosen you out of the world, therefore the world hateth you" (John 15:19). We can expect opposition and difficulty. Sadly, that sometimes comes not from the world but from other believers who should be standing and serving with us, but who oppose us instead.

In either case, God is looking for people who cannot be stopped, who will serve no matter what happens. These are the faithful ones who are willing to pay the price to do what God has called them to do. While the world may never recognize or reward them, God considers them worthy of His praise and approval.

—— Today's Renewal Principle ——

When we are faithful to serve God regardless of the immediate results, He will provide eternal rewards.

Restoring Grace

Simon Peter said unto him, Lord, whither goest thou? Jesus answered him, Whither I go, thou canst not follow me now; but thou shalt follow me afterwards. Peter said unto him, Lord, why cannot I follow thee now? I will lay down my life for thy sake. Jesus answered him, Wilt thou lay down thy life for my sake? Verily, verily, I say unto thee, The cock shall not crow, till thou hast denied me thrice.—**John 13:36–38**

Peter had complete confidence in himself—far more than was warranted. He adamantly declared that, if all of the other disciples abandoned Jesus, he would remain faithful. Peter did not take into account Satan's desire to destroy him, nor did he understand his own weakness. When the moment of truth came, Peter failed the test. He fled with the other disciples when Jesus was arrested, and he denied being a follower of Jesus three times.

Despite all of his boasting, Peter proved unequal to the challenge. Yet, rather than condemning Peter, Jesus came to him by the shores of Galilee and gave him an assignment for ministry and service that would last the rest of Peter's life (John 21:19). Just weeks later, the restored disciple preached with boldness and power a message that he knew firsthand—that there is grace for those who repent and turn to Jesus (Acts 2).

Later on in his life, when the Holy Spirit inspired him to write his first letter to Christians scattered around the world, Peter must have remembered that moment. He wrote, "Likewise, ye younger, submit yourselves unto the elder. Yea, all of you be subject one to another, and be clothed with humility: for God resisteth the proud, and giveth grace to the humble" (1 Peter 5:5). Instead of proudly clinging to our sin, trying to downplay or justify it, we need to be people who acknowledge our need of grace and seek God's forgiveness and restoration.

—— Today's Renewal Principle ——

God's grace is sufficient to bring us back into fellowship with Him regardless of our failures.

Finding Joy in God

*I will greatly rejoice in the LORD, my soul shall
be joyful in my God; for he hath clothed me with
the garments of salvation, he hath covered me
with the robe of righteousness, as a bridegroom
decketh himself with ornaments, and as a bride
adorneth herself with her jewels. For as the
earth bringeth forth her bud, and as the garden
causeth the things that are sown in it to spring
forth; so the Lord GOD will cause righteousness
and praise to spring forth before all the nations.*
—Isaiah 61:10–11

Everything that we have in this life is temporal
and fleeting. No matter how careful we are to
exercise and eat right, our health can be lost in a
moment. Even if we are wise with our finances,
an unexpected reversal beyond our control can
wipe out everything we have gained. Friends can
move, or relationships can be broken. Family
relationships can be strained, and those we love
may go to Heaven before us. If we are seeking our

source of joy in any of these things, we are doomed to disappointment.

We serve a God, however, who never fails and never changes. James 1:17 says, "Every good gift and every perfect gift is from above, and cometh down from the Father of lights, with whom is no variableness, neither shadow of turning." If the focus of our lives is on Him—the grace and goodness that He has freely given to us and the wonderful promises that are ours to claim—we will find a source of joy that will never be lost. The knowledge of God's unchanging love has sustained His children through the ages even during the most difficult circumstances. In every kind of distress, Christians can find joy when they are focused on Jesus, the source of all true joy.

—— Today's Renewal Principle ——

If you are in need of joy today, spend time focused on all that God is and has done for you instead of on your problems.

No Fear of Man

And others had trial of cruel mockings and scourgings, yea, moreover of bonds and imprisonment: They were stoned, they were sawn asunder, were tempted, were slain with the sword: they wandered about in sheepskins and goatskins; being destitute, afflicted, tormented; (Of whom the world was not worthy:) they wandered in deserts, and in mountains, and in dens and caves of the earth.—**Hebrews 11:36–38**

A mong the many notables buried at Westminster Abbey in London is the body of John Laird Mair Lawrence, the first Lord Lawrence. The son of an Army officer, Lawrence devoted his life to serving his country. Nearby, his grave is a marble bust of Lawrence with an inscription detailing his many years of service to the British crown as Viceroy of India and the love of his family. Included are these powerful words: "His devotion to public duty was ennobled by the simplicity and purity of his private life. 'He feared Man so little, because he feared God so much.'"

God does not promise us an easy life of comfort. There are times when doing right is exactly what leads to persecution and trouble. In those moments we are tempted to lower our sails—to take a quieter stand, to stop doing the things that are causing us problems. Of course, in cases where the trouble is a result of wrongdoing, we should change. But when we are suffering for righteousness' sake, we should remain steadfast and unmovable.

The early disciples faced great persecution because they would not stop preaching about Jesus, yet when they were beaten and threatened, they remained faithful. Acts 5:41 says, "And they departed from the presence of the council, rejoicing that they were counted worthy to suffer shame for his name." We should never let anything deter us from doing what we know is right.

—— Today's Renewal Principle ——

When we fear God as we should, we won't fear man as we shouldn't.

Brotherly Love

But as touching brotherly love ye need not that I write unto you: for ye yourselves are taught of God to love one another. And indeed ye do it toward all the brethren which are in all Macedonia: but we beseech you, brethren, that ye increase more and more;—**1 Thessalonians 4:9–10**

O ne of the early groups with a strong focus on missions were the Moravians. It is said that during the 1700s, a dispute arose between two factions within the group. A leader of the movement, Count Zinzendorf, called the two sides together for a conference. They began on a Monday morning, not with an airing of their differing opinions, but with a study of First John and its teaching on loving other believers. All week long they read, prayed, and studied that short book from the Bible. On Sunday they held their regular services, then the next day began meeting to discuss the argument, only to reach an agreement in a matter of minutes. Love overcame their differences.

Many of the conflicts that arise in our churches and families could be overcome by a renewed focus on our love for God. When an orchestra plays together, if each instrument is tuned by its own standard, discord will be the result. When they are all tuned to the same instrument, beautiful music follows. The presence of strife and disagreement shows that our love for each other, which is based on our love for God, needs to be strengthened.

Because we all have fallen natures, it is certain that disputes will arise and disagreements will come. Love does not prevent differences of opinion, but it does govern our responses to them. Love prevents our disagreements from becoming divisions that weaken the body of Christ and reduce its power. Love reaches out and seeks the best for the other person.

—— Today's Renewal Principle ——

When our hearts are in tune with God and we love Him as we should, it is easy for us to love other believers.

Bring the Lost to Jesus

One of the two which heard John speak, and followed him, was Andrew, Simon Peter's brother. He first findeth his own brother Simon, and saith unto him, We have found the Messias, which is, being interpreted, the Christ. And he brought him to Jesus. And when Jesus beheld him, he said, Thou art Simon the son of Jona: thou shalt be called Cephas, which is by interpretation, A stone.—**John 1:40–42**

Andrew is not someone we think of as a major Bible character. Outside of the places where his name is included as part of a list of the disciples, he only appears in three stories. Yet, in each of those stories, Andrew is found bringing someone to Jesus. What a wonderful testimony for anyone to have. There is no more important calling that we have as Christians than to share our faith with a lost and dying world. The world has many different standards by which success is measured, but they are all focused on temporal things. God is interested in the eternal, and He calls us to go out with the gospel and win the lost.

J.B. Chapman said, "Young man, young woman, make the most of your life. Go after souls. Go after them the best way you know, but go after them. Do not listen to those who warn you that you will offend and drive away by your persistence. Go after souls. Go after them by public and private testimony. Go after them by service and by prayer. But go after them. Go after them with love and a burdened heart. Go after them by kind deeds. Go after them by song and praise. Go after them when they are bereaved and in sorrow. Go after them when they are especially favored of God and men. But go after them. This soulwinning life is your life, make the most of it."

—— Today's Renewal Principle ——

If it can be said of you that you brought others to Jesus, your life has been a success in God's eyes.

Gracious Words

Withal praying also for us, that God would open unto us a door of utterance, to speak the mystery of Christ, for which I am also in bonds: That I may make it manifest, as I ought to speak. Walk in wisdom toward them that are without, redeeming the time. Let your speech be alway with grace, seasoned with salt, that ye may know how ye ought to answer every man.—**Colossians 4:3–6**

Nathaniel Hawthorne, considered one of America's greatest authors, was not widely accepted in his early career, and had to find additional ways to support his family. He worked in the customs house in Salem, but a change in political administration meant that he was fired along with all those who had supported the opposing side. When Hawthorne returned home to give his wife the bad news, she simply said, "Now you can write your book." Hawthorne began his work on *The Scarlet Letter*, a book that established his place in literary circles, because of words of encouragement.

It is not hard to find people who will point out the problems and difficulties you face and the things others are doing wrong to you. One author referred to them as the "Discouragement Fraternity." But how refreshing and wonderful it is to hear encouragement from a friend or family member when things are tough! The power of our words cannot be overstated.

Too often, when speaking harshly, we fall back on the excuse that we are speaking the truth, forgetting the admonition to season our words with grace. While we should always tell the truth, not everything that is true needs to be said in every circumstance. Sometimes people who are carrying a heavy load just need a kind word of hope and encouragement to keep going. Those who encourage others truly have a great ministry.

—— Today's Renewal Principle ——

Choose your words today with care to ensure that they are filled with grace and encouragement for others.

Persistence in Prayer

And he said unto them, Which of you shall have
a friend, and shall go unto him at midnight, and
say unto him, Friend, lend me three loaves; For a
friend of mine in his journey is come to me, and
I have nothing to set before him? And he from
within shall answer and say, Trouble me not: the
door is now shut, and my children are with me
in bed; I cannot rise and give thee. I say unto you,
Though he will not rise and give him, because he
is his friend, yet because of his importunity he
will rise and give him as many as he needeth.
–Luke 11:5–8

George Müller said, "The great fault of the children of God is that they do not continue in prayer; they do not go on praying; they do not persevere. If they desire anything for God's glory, they should pray until they get it."

Müller's own life is a great testimony to the power of persistent prayer. For decades, he ran orphanages caring for thousands of children, with all of the financial needs being met through prayer. Before his conversion, Müller had been a godless young man; after he was saved, he began praying for the salvation of his friends from those days. For more than fifty years, Müller prayed specifically for five of them. Four were saved over the years of his prayers (one of these shortly before his death), and the final friend was saved within months of his passing into Heaven. Though the answer was long delayed, Müller never gave up on the power of prayer.

There are cases where God clearly closes a door or changes the desires of our hearts. But until and unless that happens, we should continue to pray in faith, even though we have not yet received what we ask God to provide.

—— Today's Renewal Principle ——

Never stop praying until either your answer comes or God changes your prayer.

Serving God in Faith

But blessed are your eyes, for they see: and your ears, for they hear. For verily I say unto you, That many prophets and righteous men have desired to see those things which ye see, and have not seen them; and to hear those things which ye hear, and have not heard them.—**Matthew 13:16–17**

Through the centuries, men and women have followed God in faith. Often they had only small portions of the Scriptures; many had no written revelation at all. Yet, through all those years, they faithfully obeyed what God told them. Sometimes, like Noah or Daniel, they stood almost alone against everyone else around them. Sometimes, like Abraham or Moses, they set out to do things that were impossible. Sometimes, like Nehemiah or Esther, they risked their lives to do what was right.

None of these people had the resources we have available to us today. In fact, they never fully realized what God's plan was. Hebrews 11:13

says, "These all died in faith, not having received the promises, but having seen them afar off, and were persuaded of them, and embraced them, and confessed that they were strangers and pilgrims on the earth."

There will always be excuses for why we cannot serve God as we should. The devil is delighted to offer us reasons to defer our labor for the Lord. Yet there is great blessing for those who take the things that they have received and put them to work in God's business. God has given us all that we need for His work through His Word and the indwelling Holy Spirit. We are not expected to do things in our own power—it is actually impossible to serve God that way. Instead we are told to rely on what He has provided and operate in the confidence that He will make a way for us.

—— Today's Renewal Principle ——

You and I are fully equipped by God's Word and His Spirit to faithfully serve the Lord today.

Charting a Consistent Course

And now, behold, I go bound in the spirit unto Jerusalem, not knowing the things that shall befall me there: Save that the Holy Ghost witnesseth in every city, saying that bonds and afflictions abide me. But none of these things move me, neither count I my life dear unto myself, so that I might finish my course with joy, and the ministry, which I have received of the Lord Jesus, to testify the gospel of the grace of God.—**Acts 20:22–24**

We have our own lives to live, and God calls us to be faithful in them. But our faithfulness is about far more than just our own lives. We are also creating a legacy that in some ways is more important and lasting than anything we do while we are alive. God's plan is for the Christian faith to be passed, not just from person to person, but from generation to generation.

Charles Spurgeon said, "If the Lord does not speedily appear, there will come another generation, and another, and all these generations will be tainted and injured if we are not faithful to God and to His truth today. We have come to a turning-point in the road. If we turn to the right, mayhap our children and our children's children will go that way; but if we turn to the left, generations yet unborn will curse our names for having been unfaithful to God and to His Word."

Think of what happened to the Children of Israel after Joshua and the men who served with him were gone. Though they served God and fought battles, they failed to transfer a real and active faith to the next generation. "And also all that generation were gathered unto their fathers: and there arose another generation after them, which knew not the Lord, nor yet the works which he had done for Israel" (Judges 2:10).

—— **Today's Renewal Principle** ——

The impact of our lives on the future should influence every decision and choice that we make.

The Great Joy of Soulwinning

And when he hath found it, he layeth it on his shoulders, rejoicing. And when he cometh home, he calleth together his friends and neighbours, saying unto them, Rejoice with me; for I have found my sheep which was lost. I say unto you, that likewise joy shall be in heaven over one sinner that repenteth, more than over ninety and nine just persons, which need no repentance.
—Luke 15:5–7

I'm thankful for the many pleasures the Lord gives us, including sports, hunting, and good meals. But I want to find my greatest joy in what initiates the cheers of Heaven, the salvation of a lost soul, and I want to focus my energy in leading that soul to Christ. I want my heart to reflect the heart of the Good Shepherd who will "go after that which is lost, until he find it…And when he hath found it, he layeth it on his shoulders, rejoicing" (Luke 15:4–5).

We speak of soulwinning as an obligation and a commandment to fulfill, and it is. But soulwinning is so much more than that; it is also a source of great joy. Heaven rejoices when a lost soul is saved. Jesus said, "Likewise, I say unto you, there is joy in the presence of the angels of God over one sinner that repenteth" (Luke 15:10). The measure of God's love for the world seen in the gift of His Son to purchase our redemption makes it easy to understand why Heaven celebrates salvation. It is the fulfillment of God's purpose.

But there is also great joy on Earth. As a parent, the days when our children were saved were some of the happiest of our lives. Those who have prayed for years for the salvation of a family member know the rejoicing that comes when those prayers are finally answered. We should not miss out on this wonderful source of joy by failing to witness.

—— Today's Renewal Principle ——

You will never do anything that brings greater joy both on Earth and in Heaven than to lead someone to Jesus.

Where Are the Nine?

And one of them, when he saw that he was healed, turned back, and with a loud voice glorified God, And fell down on his face at his feet, giving him thanks: and he was a Samaritan. And Jesus answering said, Were there not ten cleansed? but where are the nine?—**Luke 17:15–17**

In September of 1860, the *Lady Elgin* left Chicago carrying several hundred people who had come to hear a speech by presidential hopeful Stephen Douglas. In a strong storm, the ship was struck by the *Augusta* and badly damaged. The captain attempted to return the vessel to shore, but the ship broke up and sank. Only one lifeboat was able to reach land safely, and the alarm was sounded. With hundreds of people clinging to wreckage, an effort was made to save them.

Edward Spencer, a young man studying for the ministry at Northwestern University, dashed out into the rough water and began bringing people back to shore. Again and again, he went out despite warnings from his friends. As his body weakened, he made one last trip, rescuing the eighteenth passenger before collapsing. He never fully recovered and remained an invalid the rest of his life. Some years later, a reporter doing a retrospective on one of the deadliest shipping accidents in United States history visited Spencer to talk about that morning. He asked if any of those Spencer had saved had returned to thank him. "Not one ever came back," Spencer replied.

Those of us who have trusted Christ were headed for Hell when God saved us. Too often we fail to stop and acknowledge the incredible gift we have received through His grace. We forget to thank God for laying down His life for us and develop a sense of entitlement of God's gracious blessings. Like nine of the ten lepers Jesus healed, we simply forget to give God thanks.

—— **Today's Renewal Principle** ——

Never let a single day go by without thanking God for His goodness and for your salvation.

Finish the Job

*Wherefore, my beloved, as ye have always obeyed,
not as in my presence only, but now much more
in my absence, work out your own salvation with
fear and trembling. For it is God which worketh
in you both to will and to do of his good pleasure.
Do all things without murmurings and disputings:*
—Philippians 2:12–14

Salvation is freely provided to us by God's grace,
but God has given us commands for how He
wants us as His children to live. One of those is
that we "work out" our salvation—not working
to obtain salvation, but rather to accomplish the
full purpose of our maturity and growth in grace.
Just as a student may be tasked with working out
a math problem by revealing all of the steps taken
to reach the answer, God wants us to carry our
salvation to its conclusion here on Earth.

Even before we were saved, God had in
mind specific things that He purposed for us
to accomplish. Paul wrote, "For we are his

workmanship, created in Christ Jesus unto good works, which God hath before ordained that we should walk in them" (Ephesians 2:10). Because each of us have specific gifts, talents, and abilities, there are things in God's kingdom which we are best suited to accomplish. No one else can do for God exactly what you can do. If we do not do what we should, the cause of Christ will be harmed.

The Greek word translated "work out" is both active and continuous in nature. It is not a one-time thing or a short-term commitment. God's plan for us to do His work continues until we reach Heaven. At every stage of our lives, we have unique things to offer the body of Christ, and we need to be sure that out of our gratitude for God's gift of salvation we do His work..

—— Today's Renewal Principle ——

As long as we are living, God has tasks which we are to accomplish for His glory.

I Cannot Make It Otherwise

*Much more then, being now justified by his blood,
we shall be saved from wrath through him. For
if, when we were enemies, we were reconciled to
God by the death of his Son, much more, being
reconciled, we shall be saved by his life. And not
only so, but we also joy in God through our Lord
Jesus Christ, by whom we have now received the
atonement.*—**Romans 5:9–11**

Franz Joseph Haydn was a giant of the music
world. He is sometimes called the "Father
of the Symphony." In addition to being a gifted
composer, he was a friend of Mozart and one of
Beethoven's teachers. His influence was vast, and
today he is primarily remembered for his classical
compositions. Yet, Haydn also wrote a great volume
of church music. In contrast to much of the style
of his day, Haydn's work had a notably cheerful
tone. Asked about the difference he replied, "I
cannot make it otherwise; I write according to the
thoughts I feel. When I think upon God my heart

is so full of joy that the notes dance and leap, as it were, from my pen; and since God has given me a cheerful heart, it will be pardoned me that I serve Him with a cheerful spirit."

One of the great needs of our day is a renewed appreciation for the amazing blessings God has given to each of us. It is easy for us to focus on what others have and discount our blessings. We live in a culture of discontent and too often take the physical, spiritual, and material blessings that we have for granted. If we take the time to stop and reflect on God's bountiful goodness given to us completely because of His grace rather than because we deserve it, we would not find it so difficult to find joy in our hearts.

—— Today's Renewal Principle ——

It is impossible for a heart that is truly grateful for God's grace not to be filled with joy.

Having a Passion for People

And unto the Jews I became as a Jew, that I might gain the Jews; to them that are under the law, as under the law, that I might gain them that are under the law; To them that are without law, as without law, (being not without law to God, but under the law to Christ,) that I might gain them that are without law. To the weak became I as weak, that I might gain the weak: I am made all things to all men, that I might by all means save some. —**1 Corinthians 9:20–22**

In the days of William Booth (1829–1912), few churches had interest in reaching the outcasts of society who lived in poverty or on the streets. After the Salvation Army was founded and began to see many lives transformed, Booth became a well-known figure in both England and America. At one point, he was invited to meet with Queen Victoria who asked him what the secret of his success was. Booth replied, "Your Majesty, some men have a passion for money. Some people have a passion for things. I have a passion for people."

We all get the same amount of time each day. The question is how we will use it. Will we spend the most precious resource that we have on the temporal or on the eternal? The Apostle Paul reminds us that we have a choice in our lives. "Now if any man build upon this foundation gold, silver, precious stones, wood, hay, stubble" (1 Corinthians 3:12). Works that are burned up at the Judgment Seat will not produce rewards. Only if we spend our time and resources on what matters to God will we hear Him say, "Well done."

Because of the eternal realities of heaven and hell and because every person is born with an eternal soul, we should invest our time, energy, and affection in making the gospel known to people. This is the passion of God's heart and one He will bless in ours.

—— Today's Renewal Principle ——

We have one life to invest in eternal things. Make sure what you do counts for God.

Giving Account

Wherefore we labour, that, whether present or absent, we may be accepted of him. For we must all appear before the judgment seat of Christ; that every one may receive the things done in his body, according to that he hath done, whether it be good or bad. Knowing therefore the terror of the Lord, we persuade men; but we are made manifest unto God; and I trust also are made manifest in your consciences.—**2 Corinthians 5:9–11**

Before he died in January of 1956, Jim Elliot was virtually unknown. But the circumstances of his death, being martyred along with four other missionaries working to reach tribes deep in the jungles of Ecuador, quickly made him a household name. Elliot was deeply committed to the cause of reaching people with the gospel. In his journal, he wrote, "Father, make of me a crisis man. Bring those I contact to decision. Let me not be a milepost on a single road; make me a fork, that men must turn one way or another on facing Christ in me." Though Jim and the other four missionaries could have defended themselves with their guns, they chose to lay down their lives. In the following years, other missionaries, including the wives of some of those men, did reach the local people with the gospel, and many were saved.

There is a level of commitment and intensity that characterizes fruitful soulwinners. They do not approach the task of sharing the gospel with a casual attitude but with a recognition of the seriousness of the cause. Not only is the eternal destiny of those to whom we witness at stake, but we will also face a day at the judgment seat of Christ when we will give an account of our faithfulness to proclaim the gospel. As Jim Elliot so rightly stated, "He is no fool who gives what he cannot keep to gain what he cannot lose."

—— Today's Renewal Principle ——

Knowing that we will one day face God to give an account should inspire us to be faithful to witness.

Prayers for Help

*Likewise the Spirit also helpeth our infirmities:
for we know not what we should pray for as we
ought: but the Spirit itself maketh intercession
for us with groanings which cannot be uttered.
And he that searcheth the hearts knoweth
what is the mind of the Spirit, because he
maketh intercession for the saints according
to the will of God.*—**Romans 8:26–27**

We often pray and do not know exactly what or
how to pray. There are times when the need
and the answer seem clear, but many times we are
left without a sense of direction or certainty. When
we pray, we know that we need to ask according to
God's will, but there are times when that is hard
for us to discern. In these moments, the most
important thing to remember is that we still must
pray. God knows our limitations and weaknesses.
Even when we do not know what is best for us or
how to pray, He steps in and, in mercy and grace,
gives us what we need. A halting and uncertain
prayer is vastly superior to one that is never offered.

In his lengthy narrative poem on the passing of England's fabled King Arthur, *Morte D'Arthur*, Alfred, Lord Tennyson wrote:

More things are wrought by prayer than this world dreams of:
For what are men better than sheep or goats
If, knowing God, they lift not hands of prayer
Both for themselves and those who call them friend.

If we do not lift our hands in prayer, we are forfeiting not just the help that we receive through prayer, but the help that God gives us to shape and mold our prayers and desires through His Holy Spirit. There are times when the process of praying and listening to God's voice is far more important than the immediate answer to our prayers.

—— Today's Renewal Principle ——

As we cry out to God for help, we need to listen to His Spirit and yield our desires to His.

Day
81

A Source of Help in Trouble

Offer unto God thanksgiving; and pay thy vows unto the most High: And call upon me in the day of trouble: I will deliver thee, and thou shalt glorify me. But unto the wicked God saith, What hast thou to do to declare my statutes, or that thou shouldest take my covenant in thy mouth?—**Psalm 50:14–16**

On July 18, 1965, Jeremiah Denton was shot down over North Vietnam. For almost eight years, he was held in captivity under extremely harsh conditions. During a television interview by his captors, he sent out a message by repeatedly blinking in Morse code to reveal that he and his fellow captives were being tortured. But his time in prison took a severe toll on him. At one point, he felt he was about to break. Denton wrote the following in his memoir: "I broke down and cried and since that time I've learned that if you do that, turn yourself over to God and say, 'Look, You be the origin of the stimuli for my thoughts, for my actions and make it be in accordance with Your will,' it's amazing how that will work."

Like an individual, a nation in trouble needs to seek God as its source of strength and help. Those who recognize the problems of our culture are often uncertain as to the best way to solve them. The reality is that there are no lasting political, economic, or legal solutions to moral problems. What we need is a revival of faith in the hearts of Christians so we will live as God directs regardless of what those around us do, and we need faith to seek God's help, not so that our lives will be easy but so that we will do right. If God's people act in His power, His help will be their strength.

Whether the trouble you may find yourself in now is personal or corporate, small or large, remember that God is your only true source of help. So call out to Him in faith.

—— Today's Renewal Principle ——

The only unfailing source of help in times of trouble is found when we cry out to God for deliverance.

82

What Fills Our Mouths?

And be not drunk with wine, wherein is excess;
but be filled with the Spirit; Speaking to
yourselves in psalms and hymns and spiritual
songs, singing and making melody in your
heart to the Lord; Giving thanks always for all
things unto God and the Father in the name of
our Lord Jesus Christ;—**Ephesians 5:18–20**

Wilbur Nelson wrote this about one of the
best-known and most effective politicians
in early America and how he interacted with his
constituents: "When Daniel Webster wanted to
give a person the impression that he remembered
him, but could not recall his name or where they
had met before, he would ask, 'Well, how is the old
complaint?' And nine times out of ten this worked.
The person would begin to unfold some grievance
that he had discussed with Mr. Webster on a former
occasion, and thereby identify himself."

The reality is that there are always things about
which we could complain. None of us have perfect
lives. All of us deal with disappointment, failure,

164   90-DAY DEVOTIONAL

and pain, yet we have a choice. Problems do not require that we spend our lives complaining and bemoaning our circumstances. Our mouths can be filled with praise and joy and words that bring glory to God no matter what is going on around us. On the day when he lost all of his possessions, Job said, "The Lord gave, and the Lord hath taken away; blessed be the name of the Lord" (Job 1:21).

When we are walking in the Spirit, one of the evidences will be seen in what comes out of our mouths. Do we sing with joy and give thanks, or do we murmur and complain? Do we appreciate what we have, or do we constantly gripe about what is lacking? It is impossible for a grateful heart and a complaining mouth to coexist. Our words should show appreciation for what God has given us.

—— Today's Renewal Principle ——

Let us be identified by joyful words and consistent praise to our God rather than by constant complaining.

A Restraining Grace

What shall we say then? Shall we continue in sin, that grace may abound? God forbid. How shall we, that are dead to sin, live any longer therein? Know ye not, that so many of us as were baptized into Jesus Christ were baptized into his death? Therefore we are buried with him by baptism into death: that like as Christ was raised up from the dead by the glory of the Father, even so we also should walk in newness of life.—**Romans 6:1–4**

People have been struggling with understanding grace for a long time. The arguments made today that people can live any way they want because of grace are not new. In fact, they go all the way back to the early church. One of the primary reasons that Paul left Titus to pastor in Crete was the false teaching about grace that had infected the believers there. Paul wrote that Titus was to "set in order the things that are wanting" (Titus 1:5). The new Christians on Crete needed grace not just for salvation, but for daily living according to God's Word.

Then, as now, there are some who would turn grace into license, teaching that Christians can live in sin since they are no longer under the law. It is true that the believer is not under the law but under grace. Grace, however, brings an even greater responsibility: how can the Christian deliberately sin against the grace and kindness of God?

Paul told Titus by inspiration that God's grace does not teach license, but restraint. The lesson of grace is that "denying ungodliness and worldly lusts, we should live soberly, righteously, and godly, in this present world" (Titus 2:12). In other words, grace *restrains* us. It gives us the power to say "no" to sin and "yes" to godliness. There is a great need today for Christians who will allow God's grace to transform their lives from the inside out.

—— Today's Renewal Principle ——

If we are not living holy lives, we are not truly living under grace.

A Source of Confidence

I know thy works: behold, I have set before thee an open door, and no man can shut it: for thou hast a little strength, and hast kept my word, and hast not denied my name. Behold, I will make them of the synagogue of Satan, which say they are Jews, and are not, but do lie; behold, I will make them to come and worship before thy feet, and to know that I have loved thee. Because thou hast kept the word of my patience, I also will keep thee from the hour of temptation, which shall come upon all the world, to try them that dwell upon the earth.—**Revelation 3:8–10**

I read about a little boy whose mother asked him to go down to the cellar and get a jar of tomato sauce. As he looked into the dark cellar, his little heart was afraid of what might be lurking unseen below. His mother said, "Don't be afraid. Jesus will be with you in the basement." The boy looked at her for a second, then yelled down the stairs, "Jesus, would You please hand me the jar of tomato sauce?"

There are many challenges that we face where we must look into the darkness, not immediately seeing how God will resolve the problem. In those moments, we need a strong and real sense of God's presence. We need to remember that He is the one who opens and shuts doors and guides our steps.

The Israelites were guided through the wilderness by a visible sign of God's presence—the pillar of cloud during the day and the pillar of fire at night (Exodus 13:21). We have something even better available to us in the written Word of God. If we use this wonderful resource rightly, we will never need to be afraid; for it will reassure us of His presence. Additionally, we have the indwelling Spirit of God. Truly, we have every reason to walk in confident assurance of God's help.

—— Today's Renewal Principle ——

When we are faced with challenges and fears, we must never forget that God is always with us.

God's Measure of Ministry

And when they were come to him, he said unto them, Ye know, from the first day that I came into Asia, after what manner I have been with you at all seasons, Serving the Lord with all humility of mind, and with many tears, and temptations, which befell me by the lying in wait of the Jews: And how I kept back nothing that was profitable unto you, but have shewed you, and have taught you publickly, and from house to house,
—**Acts 20:18–20**

When I came to Lancaster Baptist Church in 1986, there was a handful of people, and the church was in desperate financial trouble. We could have tried to resolve these troubles by focusing on stewardship or launching a giving campaign, but that did not offer much hope. I had never pastored before, though I had been on a church staff. There were a lot of things I did not know, but the one thing I knew for sure was that our community needed the gospel of Jesus Christ. So we started knocking on doors and brought witness of the gospel to thousands of homes. Eventually, God provided for the other difficulties as He built His church.

With all my heart, I believe that the purpose of the local church is summed up in the commission Christ gave His disciples just before He ascended to Heaven. This last command of Christ should be our highest priority; every facet of church activity should in some way relate to this—the purpose of the church. Acts 5:42 records that the Jerusalem church was indeed fulfilling this purpose: "And daily in the temple, and in every house, they ceased not to teach and preach Jesus Christ." This young church was constantly engaged in making the gospel known to the world. We do not need new methods today. Our great need is for obedience to God's revealed plan of soulwinning.

—— Today's Renewal Principle ——

God is not impressed with our programs and methods; He wants us to follow His command and be faithful witnesses.

We Owe a Debt

Wherefore seeing we also are compassed about with so great a cloud of witnesses, let us lay aside every weight, and the sin which doth so easily beset us, and let us run with patience the race that is set before us, Looking unto Jesus the author and finisher of our faith; who for the joy that was set before him endured the cross, despising the shame, and is set down at the right hand of the throne of God.—**Hebrews 12:1–2**

On August 20, 1940, while Britain stood almost alone against Nazi Germany, believing that a German invasion could come any day, Prime Minister Winston Churchill rose to speak to the House of Commons. After an update on the war situation, he turned to the topic of the Royal Air Force which was valiantly struggling to defend England against air attacks by the far superior German Luftwaffe. Churchill said, "The gratitude of every home in our Island, in our Empire, and indeed throughout the world, except in the abodes of the guilty, goes out to the British airmen who, undaunted by odds, unwearied in their constant challenge and mortal danger, are turning the tide of the World War by their prowess and by their devotion. Never in the field of human conflict was so much owed by so many to so few."

Christians have a history filled with heroes of the faith. We can look back on the lives of those men and women who believed the promises of God and lived according to them regardless of the cost or consequences. Even more importantly, we have the example of Jesus who faithfully followed the will of His Father, even to the cross. It is our duty to show our appreciation and gratitude for this amazing heritage by following their example and running our own race with focus and purity until we reach Heaven.

—— Today's Renewal Principle ——

To those who have walked faithfully before us, and most of all to our Saviour, we owe a great debt of gratitude.

Access to Grace

Therefore being justified by faith, we have peace with God through our Lord Jesus Christ: By whom also we have access by faith into this grace wherein we stand, and rejoice in hope of the glory of God. And not only so, but we glory in tribulations also: knowing that tribulation worketh patience; And patience, experience; and experience, hope: And hope maketh not ashamed; because the love of God is shed abroad in our hearts by the Holy Ghost which is given unto us.—**Romans 5:1–5**

If you have ever taken your family to an amusement park, you know how long the lines can be for popular rides. In an effort to streamline the process and allow visitors to spend more time enjoying the park rather than just standing in line, a number of parks have found more efficient ways to get people where they need to be at the right time. One technique is an electronic wristband that allows visitors to know when their ride times are, and to pay for food and souvenirs by simply swiping the wristband past a reader.

All of us have experienced times when better access would have been helpful. But in the spiritual realm, we have already been given all the access we need to have a relationship with God. When Jesus died on the cross, the veil in the Temple was torn apart from the top to the bottom, symbolizing that our path to God was now open.

The writer of Hebrews said, "Let us therefore come boldly unto the throne of grace, that we may obtain mercy, and find grace to help in time of need" (Hebrews 4:16). Literally, we have direct access to the throne room of Heaven. No lines. No wristbands. We simply come boldly to the throne of grace. Yet despite that wonderful offer, too many times we go it alone rather than relying on God.

Do you have need of grace in your life? You can have it! Go directly to God's throne and confidently ask for it.

—— Today's Renewal Principle ——

The problem most of us have is not a lack of access to God, but a failure to use that access.

God's Plan for Our Dark Days

Then Joseph her husband, being a just man, and not willing to make her a publick example, was minded to put her away privily. But while he thought on these things, behold, the angel of the Lord appeared unto him in a dream, saying, Joseph, thou son of David, fear not to take unto thee Mary thy wife: for that which is conceived in her is of the Holy Ghost. And she shall bring forth a son, and thou shalt call his name JESUS: for he shall save his people from their sins.—**Matthew 1:19–21**

When Joseph found out Mary was going to have a baby, his heart must have been broken. All of his hopes and dreams for the future were shattered. What he did not realize at first was that God was using a temporarily painful experience in his life as part of a much greater plan. When the angel appeared to Joseph and told him what was really going on, Joseph immediately responded in faith and obedience and did as he was told. Even though doing what God commanded brought him shame and humiliation, Joseph was willing to do it because of his faith and hope in God.

Robert Morgan wrote, "Yes, the Bible does use the word hope. But in the Bible, hope is not synonymous with maybe. Biblical hope refers to sure and certain expectations, which, because they're still in the future, create in us a sense of anticipation. We don't always feel that God's way is right, but His faithfulness doesn't depend on our vacillating emotions, rather on His unchanging Word. It's not a matter of how we feel but of what God says." All of us have days when it seems that everything goes wrong. But as long as we are walking in obedience, we have every reason to hold on to our hope.

—— Today's Renewal Principle ——

If we focus on the sovereignty of God in our lives, we find reasons to praise Him even on our darkest days.

O Worship the King

*Bless the LORD, O my soul. O LORD my God, thou
art very great; thou art clothed with honour and
majesty. Who coverest thyself with light as with
a garment: who stretchest out the heavens like a
curtain: Who layeth the beams of his chambers
in the waters: who maketh the clouds his chariot:
who walketh upon the wings of the wind: Who
maketh his angels spirits; his ministers a flaming
fire:*—**Psalm 104:1–4**

Sir Robert Grant was born in India in 1779, and
after returning to England for his education,
Grant took a seat in Parliament where he served
for a number of years before returning to India
as governor of Bombay. An ardent supporter
of mission work, Grant was also a gifted poet.
Challenged and stirred by the words of Psalm 104,
he wrote a great hymn of worship and praise:

> *O Worship the King all glorious above!*
> *O gratefully sing his power and his love,*
> *Our Shield and Defender, the Ancient of days,*
> *Pavilioned in splendor, and girded with praise.*

Frail children of dust, and feeble as frail,
In thee do we trust, nor find thee to fail;
Thy mercies how tender, how firm to the end,
Our Maker, Defender, Redeemer, and Friend.

The God of the Bible is very different from the God our culture pictures. The prophet Isaiah wrote, "In the year that king Uzziah died I saw also the Lord sitting upon a throne, high and lifted up, and his train filled the temple" (Isaiah 6:1). If we do not see God as exalted, we are not really seeing Him at all. Our world, and especially our own hearts, urgently need a vision of the true nature and character of God. We cannot grasp His greatness with our finite minds, but we can acknowledge His rightful claim as Ruler of all.

—— Today's Renewal Principle ——

The glory of God's majesty should daily call forth worship from our grateful hearts.

Keep Your Eyes on the Goal

*Not as though I had already attained, either were
already perfect: but I follow after, if that I may
apprehend that for which also I am apprehended
of Christ Jesus. Brethren, I count not myself to have
apprehended: but this one thing I do, forgetting
those things which are behind, and reaching forth
unto those things which are before, I press toward
the mark for the prize of the high calling of God in
Christ Jesus.*—**Philippians 3:12–14**

Evangelist D.L. Moody told the story of a young
student who enrolled at Amherst College.
Immediately after he moved into his dormitory,
he put a letter V over the door. Other students
questioned him about it, but he refused to explain.
As a result he endured a great deal of teasing and
ridicule, but he simply went about his business.
Four years later, he was giving the speech to the
graduating class as the class valedictorian, the word
for which his V stood. He had set a goal, overcome
obstacles, and persevered until he reached it.

If we want to accomplish meaningful and important endeavors, it is critical that we stay focused on our goals. There are always going to be distractions and obstacles along the way. Nothing of value has ever been attained without effort. The difference between people who reach their goals and those who do not is not the absence of obstacles but the commitment to overcome them.

The calling of God on our lives is a high and noble thing, and it is worthy of our pursuit and full effort. When we allow difficulty to deter us from following God, we demonstrate that we do not fully appreciate the importance of what we are meant to do for Him. In truth, God does not need us to accomplish His purposes, but He allows us to be part of His work in His grace. The work we are doing for Him deserves our very best.

—— Today's Renewal Principle ——

Focusing on what matters most allows us to overcome the obstacles and hardships to reach our goals.

INDEXES

▼

Title Index

Scripture Index

About the Author

Dr. Paul Chappell is the senior pastor of Lancaster Baptist Church and the president of West Coast Baptist College in Lancaster, California. He is a powerful communicator of God's Word and a passionate servant to God's people. He has been married to his wife Terrie for thirty-five years, and he has four married children who are all serving in Christian ministry. He enjoys spending time with his family, and he loves serving the Lord shoulder to shoulder with a wonderful church family.

Dr. Chappell's preaching is heard on *Daily in the Word*, a radio program that is broadcast across America. You can find a station listing at dailyintheword.org.

You can also connect with Dr. Chappell here:

Blog: paulchappell.com
Twitter: twitter.com/paulchappell
Facebook: facebook.com/pastor.paul.chappell

Devotionals also available from
Striving Together Publications

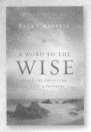

A Word to the Wise
In this power-packed daily devotional, each page shares a nugget of wisdom from the book of Proverbs. Written for the practically-minded Christian, each reading concludes with a distilled truth that you can immediately apply to your life. Let God's wisdom from the book of Proverbs equip you for the challenges of your daily life. (424 pages, hardback)

Rooted in Christ
In this daily devotional, each page beckons you to a deeper relationship with God, helping you discover for yourself the life-changing power of His unshakable love. As each brief reading draws you to the Lord, you'll be equipped to greet each day with bold faith, confident in God's faithfulness, strength, and transforming grace. (424 pages, hardback)

A Daily Word
Designed to compliment your daily devotional walk with the Lord, this book from Paul Chappell features 366 daily devotional thoughts to strengthen and encourage your spiritual life. Each devotion features a one-year Bible reading selection. Also included are helpful reference resources as well as Scripture and title indexes. (424 pages, hardback)

strivingtogether.com

Visit us online

strivingtogether.com

wcbc.edu